THE HAMLYN LECTURES

TWENTY-THIRD SERIES

PUNISHMENT, PRISON
AND
THE PUBLIC

AUSTRALIA
The Law Book Company Ltd.
Sydney : Melbourne : Brisbane

CANADA AND U.S.A.
The Carswell Company Ltd.
Agincourt, Ontario

INDIA
N. M. Tripathi Private Ltd.
Bombay

ISRAEL
Steimatzky's Agency Ltd.
Jerusalem : Tel Aviv : Haifa

MALAYSIA : SINGAPORE : BRUNEI
Malayan Law Journal (Pte) Ltd.
Singapore

NEW ZEALAND
Sweet & Maxwell (N.Z.) Ltd.
Wellington

PAKISTAN
Pakistan Law House
Karachi

PUNISHMENT, PRISON AND THE PUBLIC

An Assessment of Penal Reform in Twentieth Century England by an Armchair Penologist

BY

RUPERT CROSS, D.C.L., F.B.A.

Vinerian Professor of English Law
in the University of Oxford

Published under the auspices of
THE HAMLYN TRUST

LONDON
STEVENS & SONS
1971

Published in 1971 by
Stevens & Sons Limited of
11 New Fetter Lane in the
City of London and printed
in Great Britain by The
Eastern Press Ltd. of London
and Reading

SBN   Hardback   420 43790 8
       Paperback   420 43800 9

CONTENTS

The Hamlyn Lectures viii

The Hamlyn Trust xi

Preface xiii

Introduction xv

I. BACKGROUND AND DRAMATIS PERSONAE . . 1

  1. The Gladstone Report 1

  2. Sir Edmund Du Cane 7
     Convict Prisons 7
     Local Prisons 9
     Hard Labour 10
     The Du Cane Regime 11
     Du Cane as a penologist and a person . 13

  3. Sir Evelyn Ruggles-Brise 16
     Prison Conditions 17
     The avoidance of imprisonment . . 19
     Individualisation of punishment and
       indeterminacy of sentence . . . 22
     Ruggles-Brise as a penologist and a
       person 27

  4. Sir Alexander Paterson 29
     Career and Personality 30
     Paterson as a penologist 33

  5. Sir Lionel Fox 37

  6. Subsequent developments and other agencies
     of penal reform 41

II. PENAL REFORM, PUNISHMENT AND PRISON . . 43

  1. The meaning of penal reform . . . 43

  2. Ewing's educative theory of punishment . 47
     Education of the offender . . . 48
     Education of the community . . . 50
     Stephen 52
     Hart 54
     Priorities 55

  3. Capital and corporal punishment . . 56
     Capital punishment 57
     Corporal punishment 60

  4. Prison Conditions 62
     A day in a prisoner's life . . . 62
     Local and open prisons 66
     Training prisons 68
     Contrast with the past 68
     Grendon Underwood 78
     After-care 81
     The extent to which prison conditions
      are reformatory 83

III. THE REDUCTION AND AVOIDANCE OF IMPRISON-
    MENT AND PUNISHMENT 87

  1. The reduction of imprisonment . . . 87
     Remission 87
     Parole 90
     Length of sentences 98

  2. The avoidance of imprisonment . . . 108
     Probation and the probation officer . 109
     Suspended prison sentences . . . 112

2. The avoidance of imprisonment—*continued*
  Offenders under twenty-one . . . 116
  Senior detention centres 126
  Borstal 128
  Mentally abnormal offenders . . . 134

 Appendix 137
  Essay by a six-month trainee at Whatton
   Detention Centre—My Detention
   Centre Sentence 137
  Essay by a trainee at Huntercombe
   Borstal—A day in Borstal . . 139

IV. RECIDIVISM AND THE COMMON MAN . . . 142

 1. Recidivism 142
  Preventive detention 145
  Extended sentences 157
  Protection of the public 158
  Corrective training 161
  Three salutary lessons 163

 2. An assessment of penal reform in twentieth
  century England 167

 3. The common man's questions . . . 171
  Excessive penal reform 172
  Sentence for murder 175
  The victim 176
  Responsibility 179

 4. Incidental suggestions 185

 5. The Royal Commission on the penal system
  1964–66 188

SELECTED BIBLIOGRAPHY 191

THE HAMLYN LECTURES

1949   Freedom under the Law
            by The Rt. Hon. Lord Denning

1950   The Inheritance of the Common Law
            by Richard O'Sullivan, Esq.

1951   The Rational Strength of English Law
            by Professor F. H. Lawson

1952   English Law and the Moral Law
            by Dr. A. L. Goodhart

1953   The Queen's Peace
            by Sir Carleton Kemp Allen

1954   Executive Discretion and Judicial Control
            by Professor C. J. Hamson

1955   The Proof of Guilt
            by Dr. Glanville Williams

1956   Trial by Jury
            by The Rt. Hon. Lord Devlin

1957   Protection from Power under English Law
            by The Rt. Hon. Lord MacDermott

1958   The Sanctity of Contracts in English Law
            by Sir David Hughes Parry

1959   Judge and Jurist in the Reign of Victoria
            by C. H. S. Fifoot, Esq.

1960   The Common Law in India
            by M. C. Setalvad, Esq.

1961   British Justice: The Scottish Contribution
            by Professor T. B. Smith

1962 Lawyer and Litigant in England
by The Hon. Mr. Justice Megarry

1963 Crime and the Criminal Law
by The Baroness Wootton of Abinger

1964 Law and Lawyers in the United States
by Dean Erwin N. Griswold

1965 New Law for a New World?
by The Rt. Hon. Lord Tangley

1966 Other People's Law
by The Hon. Lord Kilbrandon

1967 The Contribution of English Law to South African
Law; and the Rule of Law in South Africa
by The Hon. O. D. Schreiner

1968 Justice in the Welfare State
by Professor H. Street

1969 The British Tradition in Canadian Law
by The Hon. Bora Laskin

1970 The English Judge
by Henry Cecil

1971 Punishment, Prison and the Public
by Professor Rupert Cross

THE HAMLYN TRUST

The Hamlyn Trust came into existence under the will of the late Miss Emma Warburton Hamlyn, of Torquay, who died in 1941, at the age of eighty. She came of an old and well-known Devon family. Her father, William Bussell Hamlyn, practised in Torquay as a solicitor for many years. She was a woman of strong character, intelligent and cultured, well versed in literature, music and art, and a lover of her country. She inherited a taste for law, and studied the subject. She also travelled frequently on the Continent and about the Mediterranean, and gathered impressions of comparative jurisprudence and ethnology.

Miss Hamlyn bequeathed the residue of her estate in terms which were thought vague. The matter was taken to the Chancery Division of the High Court, which on November 29, 1948, approved a Scheme for the administration of the Trust. Paragraph 3 of the Scheme is as follows: —

> "The object of the charity is the furtherance by lectures or otherwise among the Common People of the United Kingdom of Great Britain and Northern Ireland of the knowledge of the Comparative Jurisprudence and the Ethnology of the chief European countries including the United Kingdom, and the circumstances of the growth of such jurisprudence to the intent that the Common People of the United Kingdom may realise the privileges which in law and custom they enjoy in comparison with other European Peoples and realising and appreciating such privileges may recognise the responsibilities and obligations attaching to them."

The Trustees under the Scheme number nine, *viz.:*

Professor J. N. D. Anderson
Professor J. A. Andrews
The Rt. Hon. Lord Justice Edmund Davies
Professor P. S. James
Dr. F. J. Llewellyn
Professor F. H. Newark
Professor D. M. Walker
Professor K. W. Wedderburn
Sir Kenneth Wheare

From the first the Trustees decided to organise courses of lectures of outstanding interest and quality by persons of eminence, under the auspices of co-operating universities or other bodies, with a view to the lectures being made available in book form to a wide public.

The Twenty-Third Series of Hamlyn Lectures was delivered in November, 1971, by Professor Rupert Cross at Oxford.

J. N. D. ANDERSON,

Chairman of the Trustees.

November 1971

PREFACE

LECTURERS are all too apt to ignore the fact that the powers
of endurance of their audiences are strictly limited. Accordingly I must stress the point that this book contains a considerably elongated version of the Hamlyn Lectures for 1971
as I hope to deliver them in Oxford in late November.

The only other matter calling for comment is the sub-title.
The reason for it will be found on p. 37. It occurs to me
that a critic might say that a mere armchair penologist has
no business to be making assessments of penal reform. My
reply would be twofold. In the first place, I think that the
occasional overall summing up by a non-expert is always
helpful; secondly, although I doubt the suitability of a lawyer
as such to be a professor of criminology, I have no doubts
about the desirability of a professor of law being a student
of criminology. A criminal lawyer who confines his attention
to the criminal law to the exclusion of the theories of punishment and the treatment of offenders is a miserable specimen.

I have a number of acknowledgments to make. First and
foremost I must thank Miss June Rodgers, M.A.(T.C.D.), B.A.
(Oxon.) for assistance with research, some of which was unfortunately not used owing to last minute changes in the plan
of the lectures. I must also thank the Nuffield Foundation
for a generous grant rendering it possible for me to employ
Miss Rodgers.

My thanks are also due to the following to whom I have
been an unmitigated nuisance with persistent enquiries and
demands for assistance: Adrian Arnold, Governor of the
Huntercombe Borstal; D. O'C. Grubb, Governor of Oxford

Prison; W. R. Ritson, Warden of the Whatton Detention Centre; Rundle Harris, former Governor of Wakefield Prison; Dr. Nigel Walker, Reader in Criminology in the University of Oxford; and the members and staff of the Oxford Penology Unit.

R. C.

September 1971.

INTRODUCTION

THE first lecture is concerned with the background of penal reform in twentieth century England, and special attention is paid to the work of four Prison Commissioners.

After defining penal reform in terms of the rehabilitation and humane treatment of the offender, the second lecture deals with some aspects of the theories of punishment, the abolition of capital punishment for murder, the abolition of corporal punishment and the amelioration of prison conditions. Doubt is cast on the possibility of their being a real reformative in any save the most exceptional cases, and it is even suggested that the belief that prison could be reformative has had a baneful influence.

After discussing remission and parole, the third lecture argues for an overall shortening of prison sentences and the imposition of some limit, other than the statutory maxima, on the judge's powers with regard to the length of fixed-term sentences. A vast increase in the probation and after-care service is canvassed; it is argued that the suspended sentence should be retained, at any rate for the time being, and the lecture concludes with a discussion of the treatment of children and young persons and the mentally abnormal offender.

The final lecture begins by drawing attention to the total failure of attempts to provide special sentences for recidivists. Reference is then made to the pressing need for experimentation with regard to the treatment and training of offenders in the community. After an attempt to assess the progress of twentieth century penal reform, some matters believed to be of interest to the common man are discussed, and the lecture concludes with a plea for a new Gladstone Report.

No attempt is made to analyse the increase in crime, to suggest causes of this unfortunate phenomenon or propose remedies; I know of none.

BACKGROUND AND DRAMATIS PERSONAE

1. THE GLADSTONE REPORT

" If a prison does not succeed in deterring an offender who has
had experience of its severities from coming back to it again and
again, it is not likely to have much influence in deterring the
criminally disposed from embarking on a criminal life. On the
contrary, the spectacle of an offender going to prison for the fifth,
the tenth, the twentieth time, is calculated to encourage the
peccant materials in the population rather than to deter them."
" Detection, says the Chairman of the Prisons' Board, is becoming
more certain owing to the greater efficiency of the police. It
would certainly be comforting to believe that this was the case.
But experience of the unfortunate inaccuracies of the respected
Chairman of the Prisons' Board forbids us to place undue reliance
on his unverified opinion on any important point relating to the
movement of crime. We have only to look at some of his annual
reports placed before Parliament in order to see the extent of these
inaccuracies. In these reports we have errors in the number of
convictions running on for a series of years until they reach a
gross total of more than $2\frac{1}{2}$ millions."
" A prison system which has no effect whatever in removing the
conditions which produce the criminal, a prison system which
aggravates these conditions, is bound to fail as a deterrent agency,
it is certain to swell the ranks of the habitual criminal population.
And this is what is happening in our midst today."

THESE quotations come from an article in the *Fortnightly
Review* for April 1894. The man pilloried by it was Sir
Edmund Du Cane, first Chairman of the Prison Commission,
and the author was the Rev. Dr. W. D. Morrison, Chaplain
of Wandsworth Prison, commonly, but erroneously, supposed
to have been dismissed by Du Cane.[1] The article was

---

[1] I can only assume that there are in circulation a number of copies of
Shane Leslie's *Sir Evelyn Ruggles-Brise* which do not contain the following erratum slip to be found at p. 88 in my copy: " The statement
here said to have been made by Sir Evelyn Ruggles-Brise that the Rev.

1

entitled " Are our prisons a failure? " and it represented the culminating point of the prevailing malaise about the state of our prisons. As far back as 1890, a writer in the *Law Quarterly Review* had described the English prison system as " a manufactory of lunatics and criminals " [2]; but, by the beginning of 1894, the malaise had found expression in the popular press.

The *Daily Chronicle* published a series of articles under the title " Our dark places." [3] The local prison system was said to have broken down " entirely and utterly "; there were complaints of overcrowding (though the problem was different in nature from that of today) [4]; degrading practices such as that according to which prisoners had to face the wall on the approach of senior officials; the lonely solitary hours in the comfortless cell and the meagre diet. No doubt it was hyperbolical to say that the local prison system had broken down, and one cannot help feeling a certain sympathy for the medical officer of Wormwood Scrubs whose letter in defence of Du Cane contained the telling remark " it is not the men

Dr. Morrison was dismissed from the Prison Service is entirely mistaken. Neither at the time of his press campaign on behalf of reform in prison, nor at any other time was Dr. Morrison ever dismissed from the service. . . ." Morrison retired from the service owing to ill-health, became rector of St. Marylebone, and did not die until 1941. He received a congratulatory note from " one of the most distinguished members " of the Gladstone Committee, for having caused the committee to be appointed (see the Preface to Morrison's *Juvenile Offenders* (1896)).

[2] A. W. Renton, 6 *Law Quarterly Review* 338.

[3] January 23, 25 and 29, 1894. Common conjecture is that the articles were inspired, if not written, by Morrison. The conjecture is hardly surprising for the article of January 23 has kind words about Wandsworth prison, and alludes to the fact that only one prison chaplain had any knowledge of statistics. Although his use of them may have been questionable, it would be idle to deny that Morrison had a considerable knowledge of statistics.

[4] p. 69, *infra.*

who write most that know most." [5]   Nevertheless, the articles produced a quantity of letters with many more curses than kisses for Du Cane and his regime.

The Government took the view that an inquiry was necessary if only as a means of satisfying the public conscience and, on June 5, 1894, the then Home Secretary, Mr. Asquith, appointed the famous Departmental Committee on Prisons under the chairmanship of his under secretary, Mr. Herbert Gladstone.   The report of that Committee, signed on April 10, 1895, has been said by Duncan Fairn, head of the Prison Department from 1964–68, to have remained, until the publication in 1959 of the White Paper called " Penal Practice in a Changing Society," " the most considered statement of penal policy ever enunciated in this country." [6]   Is this a balanced assessment?   In answer to the question Mr. Fairn could take refuge in the fact that, apart from those contained in the two documents he mentions, there have been few " statements of penal policy " in this country as distinct from specific recommendations for reform.   Indeed, the Gladstone Report itself does not look at all like a statement of penal policy; but I think that, on further investigation, Mr. Fairn's assessment proves to be fully justified.

The committee's original terms of reference were certainly not conducive to broad statements of policy.   They were concerned with prison accommodation, the extent to which juvenile and first offenders should be treated as classes apart, prison labour, prison visits, prison discipline and the appointment of deputy governors.   Even the subsequent additions of the treatment of habitual criminals and the classification of prisoners can scarcely have led anyone to expect anything

[5] *Daily Chronicle*, January 29, 1894.
[6] *Changing Concepts of Crime and its Treatment* (ed. Klare), p. 160.

very breathtaking by way of formulation of principle. There is force in the comment made by Du Cane after his retirement that the instrument appointing the committee was somewhat remarkable when considered in connection with the actual report.[7]

Some of the numerous recommendations of the committee were not of the kind normally to be found in bold statements of penal policy. No doubt it was of the utmost importance that number one dietary punishment should only be inflicted when no other efficient substitute is to be found, or that a prison matron should not wear a uniform, but this is not the stuff of which epoch-making declarations are made. Other recommendations were unquestionably of the greatest prophetic significance. To take three of the most noteworthy examples, the suggested experiment of a penal reformatory for offenders above the age of sixteen and under the age of twenty-three was to develop into Borstal; the suggestion that consideration might be given to a new form of sentence by which habitual criminals would be segregated under special conditions for long periods foreshadowed preventive detention; and the proposal of an intermediate or pre-release prison was an experimental idea which is only beginning to be realised in the prison hostel system of our own time.[8] Nonetheless, I think that the main claim of the Gladstone Report to be regarded as a " considered statement of penal policy " is to be found in the enlightened dicta which can be extracted from its interstices. To my mind it is the Report's

[7] *Nineteenth Century*, Vol. 38, p. 278.

[8] See para. 91 of the Report. The system appears to have worked in Ireland, where labour was scarce, but the government "naturally shrank from the great and novel responsibility of finding employment in England for discharged convicts " (Ruggles-Brise, *The English Prison System*, p. 30).

attitude to three matters in particular which make it a land-
mark in the history of English penal reform. These matters
are the regard paid to the possibility that prison conditions
might be so contrived as to have a positive reformative effect,
the recognition of the need to ameliorate the lot of the
prisoner, and the recognition of the problem of recidivism.

The discussion of the provision of work for the inmates of
local prisons begins with the much quoted words " in the
consideration of this question we start with the principle that
prison treatment should have as its primary and concurrent
objects, deterrence and reform." [9] The reformatory theory
of punishment is of course as old as Plato; and, at an un-
official level, it had been recognised in English discussions of
prison treatment for the better part of a century before the
Gladstone Report was published. The novelty consisted in
the official blessing given to the reformatory aim of imprisonment and as one to rank *pari passu* with deterrence. Fifty
years earlier Lord Denman had declared the combination of
reform and deterrence as aims of imprisonment to be a
contradiction in terms.[10]

The Report recommended a number of ameliorations in
the conditions of imprisonment. These included the abolition of the treadmill, the reduction of solitary confinement,
more books, more classes and better diet. They may not
amount to much by modern standards, but the recommendations were made in 1895 and, as recently as 1863, a select
committee of the House of Lords had canvassed a regime

---

[9] Para. 47.

[10] Answer to question 23 put to the judges by the Select Committee of the
House of Lords on Juvenile Offenders and Transportation (1847). The
other judges were far less dogmatic, a fact for which inadequate
allowance is made in Ruggles-Brise, *op. cit.* p. 89.

based on hard labour, hard fare and a hard bed, supported by separate confinement and the crank.

Paragraph 15 of the Report reads:

" In proportion to the spread of education, the increase of wealth, and the extension of social advantages, the retention of a compact mass of habitual criminals in our midst is a growing stain on our civilisation. In any thorough enquiry into prison treatment, the closest regard must be paid to its physical and moral effect on prisoners generally.   But the number of habitual criminals in and out of prison must form one of the standards by which the system must be tested and judged.   Recidivism is the most important of all prison questions, and it is the most complicated and difficult."

It would be possible to pass over these statements as so many glimpses of the obvious, but it would be wrong to do so for two reasons. In the first place, there had been no previous serious consideration of the treatment of the recidivist; secondly, the problem is still with us, every bit as unsolved as it was in 1895.

Whether or not I am right in regarding the Gladstone Report's approach to the reform of the criminal, the amelioration of prison conditions and the problem of recidivism as the principal justifications of Mr. Fairn's reference to it as a considered statement of penal policy, the manner in which the Report deals with these matters has certainly prompted some of the questions to be raised in these lectures. Does a reformatory theory of punishment make sense? How far have prison conditions really improved since 1895? Does the idea of prison as a therapeutic community make sense?   How has the problem of recidivism been tackled?

These questions are going to be considered in my subsequent lectures. The rest of this lecture is devoted to the persons, statutes and institutions constituting the background of penal reform in twentieth century England. My account is based on the achievements during the period 1877–1961 of four prison commissioners, Sir Edmund Du Cane (1830–1903), Sir Evelyn Ruggles-Brise (1857–1935), Sir Alexander Paterson (1885–1947) and Sir Lionel Fox (1895–1961). In each instance there is material from which it is possible to gather something of their penology as well as their practical performance.

2. SIR EDMUND DU CANE

Du Cane became chairman of the newly created Board of Prison Commissioners in 1877 but, in order to appreciate the merits and demerits of his achievement, it is necessary to go further back into the nineteenth century. Born in 1830, he joined the Royal Engineers from which he retired in 1870 with the rank of colonel. Most of his army career was spent on prison work; he was organising convict labour in Western Australia between 1851 and 1856; in 1863 he became one of the directors of convict prisons and, in 1869, he was appointed Chairman of the Board.

Convict Prisons. Unlike local prisons which were administered by the local authorities and largely controlled by the justices, convict prisons were controlled by the central government. They were places in which sentences of penal servitude were served. The offender spent the first nine months of his sentence in separate confinement in his cell. Even his exercise took place, so far as possible, in solitude. He was able to talk to the chaplain and governor if they visited him, but, apart from chapel attendance, there was no association with other convicts. The next portion of the sentence was spent at a " public works " convict prison, Portland or Dartmoor for example. The period between the end of the day's work (say 5 p.m.) and the following morning was spent in the cell; but there was association, subject to a theoretically absolute ban on talking, at work. The convict was in due course released on licence for the residue of his sentence. The period of the release on licence was a quarter of the sentence remaining on transfer to a public works prison.[11]

Penal servitude was the successor of transportation. The release on licence derived from the " ticket of leave " granted to transported convicts either immediately on arrival in the penal settlement, or after a period of imprisonment there. The condition of the ticket of leave was work either for the government or for a free settler. The period of separate confinement with which sentences of penal servitude began also had its origins in transportation. In 1842 Pentonville Prison was built. It was primarily intended for the reception of convicts between the ages of eighteen and thirty-five sentenced to transportation for their first offence. For these men, Pentonville was to be " the portal to the penal colony." They spent eighteen months' separate cellular confinement there, but the experience was primarily intended to be reformatory. Lectures were given to the convicts in the chapel, they were taught a trade in their cells and trained to become useful members of the penal settlement.[12] Reduced to nine months, the initial period of solitary confinement was applied to all sentences of penal servitude after 1857, but, by then, greater importance was attached to its deterrent merits than

[11] Du Cane, *The Punishment and Prevention of Crime*, p. 162.
[12] See para. 77 of the Gladstone Report.

to its reformative potentialities. Hard cellular labour rather than industrial training was the order of the day.

Local Prisons. The degree of control which the central government could and should exercise over the administration of the local prisons by the local authorities had been in issue on a number of occasions during the nineteenth century. The lack of central control meant a considerable lack of uniformity in the regimes of these establishments. The two main systems of prison discipline canvassed in the second quarter of the nineteenth century were the " silent " or " associated " system and the " separate " system. Under the silent system, the prisoners slept, ate and spent their spare time in their cells, but worked together (" in association ") in the prison workshops. As the name of the system implies, talking was strictly prohibited. Under the separate system, the prisoners spent all their time in their cells, apart from time spent on exercise or at services in the chapel, on which occasions masks were worn in order to prevent recognition or communication. The predominance of cellular confinement meant that the type of work with which the prisoners could be provided was extremely limited as it had to be of a kind which could be done in the cell. Nonetheless, the separate system ultimately prevailed, although it seems to have been subject to considerable local modifications. The sentences of imprisonment, as distinct from penal servitude, were short (often for days or weeks rather than months). The belief that two years was the maximum permitted by the common law precluded anything particularly drastic so far as the length of a sentence to a local prison was concerned.[13]

---

[13] The belief turned out to be erroneous (see Cross, *The English Sentencing System*, p. 34).

Hard Labour. Statutes dating back to the eighteenth century authorised hard labour for convicted felons. The nature of the labour was defined in fairly general terms. Section 19 of the Prison Act 1865 divided hard labour into two classes. Hard labour of the first class was " the tread wheel, shot drill, crank, capstan, stone breaking, or such other hard bodily labour as may be determined by the justices with the approval of the Secretary of State." Second class hard labour was " such other description of bodily labour as might be appointed by the justices." In consequence of modifications made by the Prison Act 1877, no more than the first month of a sentence of imprisonment with hard labour had to be spent on hard labour of the first class. Thanks to a recommendation of the Gladstone Committee, this kind of hard labour was abolished by the Prison Act 1898. Rules made under that Act provided for twenty-eight days employment on hard manual or bodily labour in strict separation, after which hard labour prisoners worked in association with ordinary prisoners pursuant to what was, in effect, the reversion to the silent system recommended by the Gladstone Report. For the first month of a sentence of hard labour the prisoner had to sleep on a plank bed without a mattress. The period of separate confinement was abolished during the first war; the period without a mattress was reduced to a fortnight before the requirement was totally abolished in 1945; hard labour was abolished by the Criminal Justice Act 1948, but not before members of the judiciary had had ample opportunity of betraying their ignorance of the implications of the term. As late as 1932 a Recorder proceeded on the assumption that three years' penal servitude was a softer option than two years' imprisonment with hard labour.[14]

---

[14] *R.* v. *Jones,* 23 Cr.App.R. 208.

As far back as 1884, Du Cane had drawn attention to the comparative meaninglessness of the distinctions between penal servitude, imprisonment, and imprisonment with hard labour.[15]   Their persistence until the Criminal Justice Act 1948 came into force is by no means the sole illustration of the snail's pace with which penal reform proceeds.

The Du Cane regime.   The Prison Act 1877 brought the local prisons under the control of the central government. The Prison Commission through which that control was exercised was a separate body from the Directors of Convict Prisons but, as the directors were also commissioners, the distinction was one in name only, and the two bodies were amalgamated in 1898.

Sir Edmund Du Cane set about his task of reorganising the local prisons with the utmost competence. " Uniformity " was the order of the day and, although Du Cane's zeal on its behalf was his undoing, in the sense that it was the rigidity of the system which he created which was the cause of many of the complaints of the early 1890s, we must recognise the force of the two reasons which impelled him to his relentless course.   In the first place, the disparities in the regimes of the different local prisons were gross.   The attention of a committee of the House of Lords in 1863 was drawn to the cases of one prison at which there was the opportunity of spending 15 hours in bed and another at which the prisoners' food was supplied by the local inn.   Secondly, there is an element of injustice in the Executive's according different treatment to different prisoners.   This point was put very forcefully by Du Cane himself when writing on penal servitude.

15 *The Punishment and Prevention of Crime,* p. 159.

" A sentence of penal servitude is, in its main features, and so far as concerns the punishment, applied on exactly the same system to every person subjected to it. The previous career and character of the prisoner makes no difference to the punishment to which he is subjected, because it is rightly considered that it is for the Courts of Law who have, or should have, a full knowledge on these points to consider them in awarding sentence; and if any prisoner were subjected to harsher or milder treatment in consequence of any knowledge the prison authorities might have of his previous character, it might be thought that he would practically be punished twice over on the same account and on information much less complete than the Court of Law would have at its command. The government would always be liable to charges of showing favour to or prejudice against certain particular prisoners; and any feeling of this kind would be fraught with danger and inconvenience." [16]

I do not wish to say a word against the current practice under which some prisoners go to open prisons while others stay in the uncongenial conditions of a local prison according to the decision of the Executive; the practice is more or less inevitable in current conditions, and we have certainly not got Du Cane's faith in the knowledge possessed by the courts of law; but approval of what happens now should never be allowed to blind us to the fact that it is not absolutely just. Offenders who are supposed to be undergoing the same punishment are treated very differently.

Two further preoccupations of Du Cane were deterrence and economy. Neither of these was likely to be productive

[16] *Ibid.* pp. 158–159.

of benign prison conditions. Nonetheless, the Gladstone Committee commended his achievement, although there were reservations.

" Upon a general review of the management of English and Welsh prisons under the existing methods laid down by the legislation and regarding the treatment and condition of the prison population objectively, we consider that the long and able administration of Sir Edmund Du Cane has achieved a large measure of success." [17]

" As we have already stated, the centralization of authority has been a complete success in the direction of uniformity, discipline and economy. On the other hand, it carried with it some inevitable disadvantages. The great, and as we consider, the proved danger of this highly centralized system has been, and is that while much attention has been given to organization, finance, order, the health of the prisoners, and prison staffs, the prisoners have been treated too much as a hopeless or worthless element of the community, and the moral as well as the legal responsibility of the prison authorities has been held to cease when they pass outside the prison gates. " [18]

Du Cane as a penologist and a person. Du Cane retired at the end of April 1895, the month in which the Gladstone Report was published.

In addition to the belief in uniformity of treatment to which reference has already been made, his penology was characterised by an uncompromising acceptance of general deterrence as the dominant aim of punishment, adherence to

[17] Para. 14.   [18] Para. 23.

the view that any amelioration of his lot while in prison is something which a prisoner must earn by industry and good conduct, and the conviction that the separate system was better than the silent system. It certainly cannot be said that Du Cane was behind his times with regard to any of these views. His faith in general deterrence was shared by his stalwart opponent W. D. Morrison: " The moment a prison is made a comfortable place to live in, it becomes useless as a safeguard against the criminal classes." [19]

The technique of the carrot according to which effort is to be encouraged by initially placing the prisoner in bad conditions, and offering him the chance of slightly better conditions on terms of industry and good conduct had been a feature of penal servitude since 1863. That part of the sentence which was spent in a public works prison was divided into stages, each stage carrying with it increased privileges and the greater proximity of release on licence. A certain number of marks had to be earned before the superior stage was reached. The technique became a characteristic feature of our entire prison system. It was based on a simple and readily comprehensible principle, but it has now been abandoned to a considerable extent. The modern rule is to give the prisoner at the outset of his sentence all the privileges which formerly had to be earned and to use their possible forfeiture as the means of securing industry and good conduct.

One of Du Cane's last public statements concerned the conflict between the separate and silent systems. Speaking of the proposal of the Gladstone Committee that association for industrial work should be extended gradually throughout the local prisons, he said:

[19] Preface to *Crime and its Causes* (1891), p. ix.

" It is to be sincerely hoped that those who have the decision on these matters may long pause before taking such a fatal step backwards as to reintroduce the associated system contrary to the well considered judgment of the best informed authorities in our own and all other countries." [20]

Those in charge did not pause for very long. The associated system was soon reintroduced into local prisons. The objection to it was based on the risk that the prisoners would contaminate each other, but that risk was taken every day in public works convict prisons. It was thought that the bad effects of substantially uninterrupted cellular confinement and the desirability of well organised prison industry made the risk one that had to be taken. In any event, it is possible that the risk of contamination is nothing but a bogy of nineteenth century penology. This is something about which we know very little. If the risk really is a bogy, a great deal of effort has been wasted during the twentieth century in the matter of the classification of prisoners. Whether his fears of the outcome of the abolition of the separate system were justified or not, Du Cane had the support of William Tallack, the secretary of the Howard Association, the predecessor of the Howard League for Penal Reform, who spoke of the " pernicious retrogression against separation " in a letter to *The Times* of April 25, 1895, which was full of praise for the retiring chairman of the Prison Commission. It is unfortunate that the best known description of Du Cane as a person comes from his successor.

" He was a courteous gentleman of the old school and, on any question of departmental governance, unless one

20 *Nineteenth Century*, Vol. 38, p. 292.

trod on his toes, of a hearty and cordial manner to all
his colleagues. . . . I unfortunately did tread on his toes
and I cannot remember that he ever spoke to me
again." [21]

3. SIR EVELYN RUGGLES-BRISE

The author of these words was Evelyn Ruggles-Brise (1857–
1935), intellectually the most interesting of the four Prison
Commissioners I am considering. He was educated at Eton
and Balliol, got a First in Greats and passed sixth into the
Civil Service. He became a Prison Commissioner in 1892
and, on Du Cane's retirement, chairman of the Commission
in 1895. He tells us that Asquith expressed a strong desire
of the government that the views of the Gladstone Committee
should, as far as practicable, be carried into execution and
that, since then, the reform and reorganisation of the prison
system proceeded in every department.[22] Some of the proposals of the Gladstone Committee could only be brought
into effect with the aid of legislation. The Prison Act 1898
was passed with this end in view, and it contained a provision
enabling the Home Secretary to make rules for the government of local and convict prisons with the result that further
legislation concerning the condition and organisation of
prisons was rendered unnecessary until 1952 when the Prison
Act, which is now in force, was passed. Other important
provisions of the Act of 1898 were the limitation on the power
to order corporal punishment for serious breaches of prison
discipline (a power which continued to exist until the Criminal
Justice Act 1967 came into force), and the provision for remission of part of the sentence for industry and good conduct in

[21] Shane Leslie, *Sir Evelyn Ruggles-Brise*, p. 89.
[22] Ruggles-Brise, *The English Prison System*, p. 77.

the case of sentences of imprisonment as distinct from penal servitude. Such a power already existed, as we have seen, in the latter case.

Prison conditions. A vast number of changes in prison conditions were effected by changes in the rules and standing orders throughout the Ruggles-Brise regime which did not come to an end until the chairman's retirement in 1921. Steps were taken to abolish the unproductive hard labour of the crank and the tread wheel even before the abolition of first class hard labour by the Act of 1898; save in the case of the first month of a sentence of imprisonment with hard labour, work in local prisons, like that in convict prisons after the initial period of separate confinement, came to be in association; the period of separate confinement with which a sentence of penal servitude began was reduced; prison diet underwent some improvements; the prisoner's bath came to be a weekly instead of a fortnightly occasion; some beneficial changes were made with regard to visits to and letters to and from prisoners; more books were allowed, and there were improvements in the training and education of prisoners.

Nevertheless, the change in prison conditions between 1895 and 1921 was in no sense a spectacular one. The convict's head was still cropped, prison clothes were still an ill-fitting " dress of shame," bespattered with broad arrows, work might be in association, but there was very little re-creation in association, and as much as seventeen hours out of the twenty-four might be spent in the cell (more still on Sundays). The silent rule was not as absolute as it had been at the time when the Gladstone Committee recommended its modification, but it must still have been extremely irksome.[23]

---

[23] Hobhouse and Brockway, *English Prisons Today*, p. 355.

Above all, the staff and the prisoners were just as remote from each other in 1921 as they had been in 1895. Unnecessary conversation between them was prohibited.

In 1919 a prison system inquiry committee was set up by the Labour Party. Its thorough deliberations lasted three years, by which time its formal connection with the Labour Party had been severed and they resulted in the comprehensive indictment of prison life comprised in Hobhouse and Brockway's *English Prisons Today*. Having been imprisoned as conscientious objectors during World War I the authors had first-hand experience of prison life, and they did not mince their words about it:

> " Self respect is systematically destroyed and self expression prevented in every phase of prison existence. The buildings in their ugliness and their monotony have a deadening and repressing effect. The labour is mostly mechanical and largely wasteful, and every indication of craftsmanship or creative ability is suppressed. The meals are distributed through momentarily open doors as though the prisoners were caged animals. The sanitary arrangements are degrading and filthy, and the dress is hideous, slovenly, and humiliating." [24]

In fairness to Ruggles-Brise and the Prison Commission it must be pointed out that an earlier commentator had said:

> " In the treatment of adult criminals of every class the limits of comfort and indulgence have been reached. It is even questionable to some capable judges whether the authorities have not gone too far." [25]

[24] *Ibid.* p. 356.
[25] Arthur Paterson, *Our Prisons*, p. 16.

These words were written in 1911 and the 1914 war was enough to prevent the period 1911–21 from being one of drastic prison reform. In fairness to Hobhouse and Brockway, however, it must be added that it is difficult to escape the conclusion that the commentator of 1911 in whose selection Ruggles-Brise played a part, was a somewhat complacent one.[26]

The avoidance of imprisonment. If the period 1895–1921 was not notable for an amelioration of prison conditions, it certainly witnessed a significant development in the avoidance of prison as a punishment and the evolution of alternative penal or corrective measures. Ruggles-Brise's role with regard to these matters was of the first importance, and he fully subscribed to the view that prison must be regarded as the last rather than the first resort.[27]

A good deal of credit for the Probation of Offenders Act 1907 must go to him. It was the first genuine probation statute in England. There had been earlier examples in the United States, but, in the course of executing an essentially jingoistic mission,[28] I must not be taken to be questioning in the slightest degree the claim that probation is of English origin. After all, it was in the 1820s that the Warwickshire magistrates sentenced juvenile offenders to a day's imprisonment, on condition that they returned to their parents or masters to be " more carefully watched and supervised in the future."

[26] p. 40, *infra.*
[27] Ruggles-Brise, *The English Prison System*, pp. 12–13.
[28] See the terms of the Hamlyn Trust. The English experimentation on the lines of probation seems to have antedated the American. The experimentation is briefly set out in the historical sketch at the beginning of the Report of the Committee on the Treatment of Young Offenders (1927 Cmd. 2831).

Probation is essentially the suspension of punishment conditional on there being no further offence for a period during which the offender is placed under personal supervision. Previous English statutes had permitted and promoted the conditional suspension of punishment but, before the Act of 1907 came into force, there was no statutory provision for supervision, although non-statutory supervision of those who were conditionally discharged might well be forthcoming from police court missionaries acting for voluntary agencies. The previous legislation had also been limited in scope for section 16 of the Summary Jurisdiction Act 1879 was confined to conditional discharges after summary trial, while the Probation of First Offenders Act 1887 only applied to first offenders. The importance of the Act of 1907 was that it allowed for conditional release by higher as well as lower courts of old lags as well as first offenders, and the person released could be placed under the supervision of one of the probation officers for whose appointment the Act expressly provided. There have been several subsequent statutory provisions concerning both probation and discharges, but they can fairly be said to have affected matters of detail alone. Although the heyday of probation was to come after his time (if it can be said to have come yet), Ruggles-Brise, writing in 1915, lamented the persistence of the belief that probation was confined to first offenders, or even to juveniles,[29] commented on the courts' failure to use probation as much as might have been expected, and looked forward to the day when each court would have its probation officer.

One of the less attractive aspects of the nineteenth century

---

[29] *The English Prison System*, pp. 109–110. Though published in 1921, much of this book appears to have been completed by 1915.

English penal system was its tolerance of the imprisonment of children although, according to the Gladstone Report, there were only 100 children under sixteen in prison on March 31, 1894.[30] The reformatory and industrial schools had undoubtedly proved of value as an alternative to imprisonment for children, but it was not until the Children Act 1908 came into force that the imprisonment of those under fourteen was totally prohibited; under the Act, imprisonment for those between fourteen and sixteen was only permitted on special certificate by the court. The effectiveness of this measure can be gauged by the fact that, whereas there were 572 receptions into prison on conviction of children under sixteen in 1907, there were only eight in 1925.[31] The present position is that no court can sentence a person under seventeen to imprisonment, and, before someone between seventeen and twenty-one can be sent to prison, the court must be satisfied that there is no other way of dealing with him.[32]

It is unlikely that Ruggles-Brise had much to do with the Children Act 1908, but there can be no doubt of his interest in and support of section 1 of the Criminal Justice Act 1914 which obliged the courts to allow time for the payment of fines. The section proved to be the most effective prison emptier that has ever got onto the Statute Book. The number of persons sent to prison in default of payment of fines fell from 55,000 in 1910 to 15,000 in 1921.[33] There has been a fair amount of subsequent legislation designed to ensure that the imprisonment of a fine defaulter should be a

---

[30] Para. 82.
[31] Report of the Committee on the Treatment of Young Offenders, p. 12.
[32] Criminal Justice Act 1948, s. 17, as amended by Criminal Justice Act 1961.
[33] Sir Lionel Fox, *English Prisons and Borstals*, p. 66.

last resort, but none of it is comparable in importance to section 1 of the Criminal Justice Act 1914. It is almost incredible that, at so recent a date, the question of whether or not a person should be sent to prison should have depended upon the availability or otherwise of a small sum of money at the moment of conviction.

Individualisation of punishment and indeterminacy of sentence. Two new penal measures were introduced by the Prevention of Crime Act 1908, Borstal training for the young offender, and preventive detention for the habitual criminal. The importance of the part played by Ruggles-Brise in these developments has never been disputed and I shall have something to say about them in my third and fourth lectures. Each of them involved elements of the individualisation of punishment and indeterminacy of sentence, subjects to which Ruggles-Brise devoted a great deal of thought. It is worth quoting two of his remarks concerning the individualisation of punishment. In the course of an address delivered to the American Prison Association in 1910 he said [34]:

> " Each man convicted of crime is to be regarded as an individual, as a separate entity or morality, who, by the application of influences of discipline, labour, education, moral and religious, backed up on discharge by a well organised system of patronage,[35] is capable of reinstatement in civic life."

In the Preface to *The English Prison System* written in 1921, he conceded that the principle that each case should be treated on its merits could be pressed too far and continued:

[34] *Prison Reform at Home and Abroad*, pp. 194–195.
[35] Ruggles-Brise's somewhat revealing word for after-care.

" But the underlying principle is sound, with a perfect prison system, based on science, we could adapt its treatment to a far greater degree than at present to the varying categories of offenders, who, under the old classical system, which recognised only the uniform and abstract type of crime and criminal, would be confined equally to the abstract and uniform type of penalty—the prison cell."

The modern variations of regime in the different types of prison would have been anathema to Du Cane although Ruggles-Brise would have approved of them; but by whom would he have wanted the individualisation of punishment to be effected, the courts or the Executive? Consideration of this point is best deferred until some of Ruggles-Brise's remarks concerning the indeterminate sentence have been quoted.

The only really indeterminate sentence is the life sentence. At the outset of such a sentence it is impossible to give the prisoner anything in the nature of an earliest possible date of release, he might be confined for the whole of his natural life, although this is extremely unlikely because the majority of lifers are released at some stage; but there are degrees of indeterminacy. The court may be obliged to impose the statutory maximum for the offence, leaving the question of release to be determined by the Executive; or the court may be empowered to fix the maximum term of incarceration, leaving it to the Executive to release the prisoner on licence at any time, or after he has served a specified portion of the term. Some people prefer to call sentences of this nature " indefinite " or " semi-indeterminate," but there is no agreed terminology.

In 1897 Ruggles-Brise paid a visit to the United States for the purpose, among others, of witnessing the different parole systems in operation. In his report on that visit he said:

> " In principle then, the ' parole system ' must be condemned. There must be a tendency to flirt with crime if the decision of the court can be set aside by a body of men, however competent, impartial and able, who rely merely on the observations of a prisoner while in prison, and upon that decide that A is a good man and can safely be discharged, B is a bad man and must be kept in custody." [36]

On the next page of the report he quotes with approval from a paper read in 1895 by a writer who is not identified:

> " The definite sentence is based upon an erroneous theory—it assumes that a judge can tell how much punishment can be imposed justly for an offence. The alternative theory that the warden of a prison can fix with accuracy the psychological moment in a criminal's career when he may be set at liberty with safety is not less erroneous and certainly more dangerous. For it is undoubtedly better, in the interests of society, that a criminal should be detained too long under an indefinite sentence than that he should be let out too soon under an indeterminate sentence."

Nonetheless, Ruggles-Brise was, throughout his official career, an advocate of the indeterminate sentence in the case of the young offender and the habitual criminal. There is, too, some evidence that he had relented in his attitude towards

[36] XIX Parliamentary Papers, p. 956 (1899).

indeterminacy of sentence in other cases. When writing about preventive detention in 1921 he said:

> " The success of the system so far as it has gone, goes far to justify a belief in the virtue of Indetermination of sentence. Public opinion may not be ripe for this yet, as applied to ordinary crime, but the principle which the system of Preventive Detention illustrates, *viz.*: —careful observation of the history, character and prospects on discharges by an Advisory Committee on the spot, with a view to the grant of conditional freedom, furnishes in a different sphere an interesting example of the value of ' individualisation.' " [37]

The above passages raise the whole question of the relations between the courts and the Executive with regard to the duration and even the nature of the punishment of convicted criminals. Du Cane would have had no truck with provisions by the Executive for variety in prison regimes.

> " The judge or court which passes the sentence should know or be able to know the exact effect of the sentence and this would be impossible if any discretion rested with the executive officers as to the mode of carrying out the punishment." [38]

In the early days of his chairmanship of the Prison Commission Ruggles-Brise was also a champion of the courts. Section 6 of the Prison Act 1898 empowered the courts to order that a sentence of imprisonment without hard labour should be spent in the first, second or third division, and if no order was made the sentence was to be spent in the third division.

[37] Preface to *The English Prison System*, p. xviii.
[38] Du Cane, *The Punishment and Prevention of Crime*, p. 159.

The effect of the rules made under the Act was that more creature comforts were available in the other two divisions. The Prison Commissioners' Report of 1900 contained the following comment:

> " The principle here given expression to is very far reaching, and, as far as we are aware, is in advance of the penal systems in force on the Continent of Europe. By it is destroyed in emphatic language, the theory that had prevailed largely hitherto, and had found expression in divers reports, *viz.* that the duty of classification is a matter for prison officials, and not for the courts of law having the individual offender and all the circumstances of his case fully detailed before it. It is obvious what an enormous responsibility is thus thrown upon courts of law, and, as we stated in our last year's report, the degree of success which this new departure may attain, must depend on the extent and manner in which courts of law realize and act upon this responsibility." [39]

Disillusionment was to come. The Report of 1910 tells us that:

> " The exercise of this power is becoming rarer still, until we are almost forced to realise that the classification aimed at by the prison reformer will not be attained by relying on the discretionary power of the courts of law." [40]

Section 1 of the Criminal Justice Act 1948 abolished the prison divisions together with penal servitude and hard labour. We now have a simple sentence of imprisonment, the length

[39] Prison Commissioners' Report 1900, para. 4.
[40] *Ibid.* 1910, para. 42.

to be fixed by the courts, the manner in which the sentence is to be served to be determined by the Executive. The introduction of parole by the Criminal Justice Act 1967 has given the Executive power to interfere with the length of sentence. There can be no doubt that the increase in the control of the Executive over the offender after he has been sentenced has been one of the major features of twentieth century penal history in this country, and Ruggles-Brise, at any rate in the latter stages of his career, would not have been opposed to it.

Ruggles-Brise as a penologist and a person. Most of his major penological ideas have already been mentioned. Nothing more need be said about his belief that prison is the last resort, his advocacy of the individualisation of punishment and his views concerning the indeterminate sentence; but a word must be added about his approach to the theories of punishment. On this matter he was an uncompromising adherent of the view that the correct order of priority is retribution, deterrence and reform. Nowhere did he state this more forcefully than in the address to the American Prison Association in 1910 to which reference has already been made; nowhere was he more explicit about his use of terms.

" By ' retributory ' of course I do not mean the vulgar and exploded instinct of vengeance or personal revenge, but the determining of the human conscience that the system of rights shall be maintained, and that he who offends against it shall be punished, and that punishment shall be of such a nature as to deter him and others from anti-social acts. By ' reformatory ' I mean the accepted axiom of modern penology that a prisoner has reversionary rights of humanity, and that these must be respected consistently with the due execution of the law, and that no effort must be spared to restore the man to society as a better and wiser man and a good citizen. Among loose thinkers and loose writers an impression seems to be gaining ground that this historic order of the factors of punishment should be inverted, and that the object of punishment should be altogether reformatory, as little as possible deterrent, and not at all retributory." [41]

Sir Lionel Fox, one of his successors as chairman of the Prison Commission, suggested that Ruggles-Brise's views with regard to the priorities of the aims of punishment account for the lack of a really substantial amelioration of prison conditions during his regime.[42] But a belief in the vindication of the system of rights is not incompatible with a determination to improve upon the 1895 standard of prison conditions. Fox tended, like so many modern penologists and criminologists, to equate retribution with "the vulgar and exploded instinct of vengeance or personal revenge." Ruggles-Brise probably had as much of the determination to improve prison conditions as could be expected of a civil servant of his generation.

His biography by Shane Leslie, a rather hastily put together little book, based in part on a brief unpublished autobiography and in part on Ruggles-Brise's second wife's reminiscences, reveals him as a man of unorthodox religious and political views. He called himself a pagan and did not believe in the House of Lords. He was regarded as an autocrat by many penal reformers, but he commanded the respect of Winston Churchill and Sir Alexander Paterson. He seems

[41] *Prison Reform at Home and Abroad*, p. 193.
[42] *English Prisons and Borstals*, p. 63.

to have been acquainted with most of the important people of his day, but, above all, he was dedicated to his work. He might have chosen as an epitaph the inscription on the gateway of the first Borstal institution:

" He determined to save the young and careless from a wasted life of crime. Through his vision and persistence, a system of repression has been gradually replaced by one of leadership and training. We shall remember him as one who believed in his fellow men."

But there would have been an alternative. At his funeral, among the large official and family wreaths, there was a small bunch of flowers inscribed:

" to the memory of a humane man, Sir Evelyn Ruggles-Brise, K.C.B. He saved me from the cat. Convict No. 2148." [43]

I wonder which of the two suggested epitaphs Ruggles-Brise would have preferred.

4. SIR ALEXANDER PATERSON

Ruggles-Brise was succeeded as chairman of the Prison Commissioners by Sir Maurice Waller; in 1928, Sir Alexander Maxwell became chairman, and he was succeeded by Sir Harold Scott in 1932. Mr. C. D. Robinson became chairman in 1938 and, in 1942, Sir Lionel Fox succeeded to the post which he held until 1960. Although Paterson was never chairman of the Prison Commissioners, it is customary to speak of the period 1922–47 as the " Paterson regime."

[43] Shane Leslie, *Sir Evelyn Ruggles-Brise*, p. 209.

Career and Personality.   Alexander Paterson (1884–1947) became a commissioner in 1922. He retired in 1945, but continued to serve in an advisory capacity until his death at the end of 1947. He was attached to the Ministry of Labour at the time of his appointment as a commissioner, but he had long been familiar with prison conditions and the penal system generally. On coming down from Oxford in 1906, he devoted his spare time to the Oxford Medical Mission to Bermondsey where he took up residence in a slum tenement. His familiarity with prison conditions was partly due to his having befriended a Bermondsey boy of eighteen who was sentenced to ten years' penal servitude for killing his teenage wife after a quarrel caused by their penury. Paterson visited the boy at Dartmoor, and the following description of the condition of the prisoners there, round about 1912, is characteristic, tendentious but nonetheless compelling:

" As I walked along the endless landings and corridors in the great cellular blocks, I saw something of the 1,500 men who were then immured in Dartmoor. Their drab uniforms were plastered with broad arrows, their heads were closely shaven, which might make them of interest to the phrenologist, but would have baffled any portrait painter. Not even a safety razor was allowed, so that in addition to the stubble on their heads, their faces were covered with a sort of dirty moss, representing the growth of hair that a pair of clippers could not remove. The prison regime, resting primarily on considerations of safe custody and security, determined to minimise the chances of violence or suicide, had succeeded in making a large number of human beings objects of contempt. No child could have recognised his father in such condition, no girl or wife believe she ever loved a man who looked like that." [44]

It is said that Paterson helped with the drafting of the Children Act 1908 [45] and, in that year, he became a director of the newly formed Borstal Association. This meant that he was responsible for the after care of youths released on licence from Borstal. In 1911 he became assistant director of the Central Association for the Aid of Discharged Prisoners. This necessitated a monthly visit to every convict prison in order to interview inmates due for discharge.

Although it would be wrong not to give due credit to Sir Maurice Waller and his successors as chairmen of the Prison Commissioners, there is no reason to doubt the statement made by Sir Alexander Maxwell, then Permanent Under Secretary at the Home Office, at the time of Paterson's death: " To his imagination and inventive force we owe almost all the schemes of penal reform which have been developed in this country in the last 25 years." [46] These schemes included a vast and continuous amelioration of prison conditions. The convict's crop and broad arrow disappeared; prison visitors were appointed for men [47]; reasonable arrangements about shaving were made; the silence rule became attenuated to the point of non-existence; a rudimentary system of prisoners' earning was inaugurated; the first open

---

44 Cited in the Preface to *Paterson on Prisons* by S. K. Ruck. The appearance of the prisoners at Dartmoor does not seem to have improved very much by the time Governor Grew arrived there in 1926 or 1927 (see Grew, *Prison Governor*, p. 39).

45 Barclay Baron, *The Doctor*, p. 164; pp. 162–165 of this book contain useful information about Paterson. It is a biography of John Stansfeld who attracted Paterson to Bermondsey.

46 Cited by Gordon Hawkins in a privately circulated appreciation of Paterson.

47 p. 65, *infra*. They had already been appointed for women.

prison came into being. What was even more important, a revolution took place in the attitude of the staff towards the prisoners under their care. Prison officers began to acquaint themselves with the prisoners' problems, and endeavoured to assist in their solution. The spirit of Paterson was embodied in rule 1 of the new Prison Rules of 1949 (now 1964): " The purpose of the training and treatment of convicted prisoners shall be to encourage and assist them to lead a good and useful life."

To Paterson must go the credit of the inauguration of the first open Borstal at Lowdham Grange in Nottinghamshire, and the method by which it was begun in the summer of 1930. A party of about forty boys, led by W. W. Llewellyn, the governor designate of Lowdham, marched there from the Feltham Borstal in Middlesex. They spent six days on the road and the march ended in the boys camping on a hillside where they began to build their own institution without cells or bars. The boys were accompanied part of the way, not only by Paterson, but also by Sir Harold Scott who returned to Whitehall fully converted to Paterson's ideas and determined to do all he could to support them.

Llewellyn has been described as a " twentieth century saint." He was only one of the many remarkable men for whose appointment Paterson was responsible. Indeed it is sometimes said that Paterson's most important contribution to penal reform was not so much the changes which were effected during his commissionership as the men he appointed to carry them out. Some of these men are still alive, and many of them, living or dead, bear testimony to the remarkable nature of his personality. In some instances those who were boys at school or very young men when they first encountered Paterson speak of the experience with the awe

appropriate to a religious conversion. Moreover, the eulogies
do not only come from his appointees, his colleagues on the
Prison Commission and those who worked with him in Toc H
or, at an earlier stage of his career, Bermondsey. Many an
ex-prisoner came to accept him as an inspired and inspiring
friend. Criticism is not lacking, particularly in relation to
the last few years of his overstrenuous career, but there is a
ring of genuine appreciation in the observation of one of the
internees he visited in Canada on behalf of the government
in 1941. " He came among us like an angel from heaven." [48]

I am solely concerned with penal reform in England, but
it would be wrong not to mention the many visits paid by
Paterson to foreign and Commonwealth prisons, often on
behalf of the Government. *Paterson on Prisons,* compiled
by S. K. Ruck, is largely based on reports of these visits, and
it is mainly on this book that one must rely when trying to
assess him as a penologist.

Paterson as a penologist. He had a gift for the aphorism
which renders him eminently quotable, but some of his utter-
ances are in danger of becoming clichés. Two of the best
known are the following:

" It is impossible to train men for freedom in a condition
of captivity." [49]

" Men come to prison as a punishment not *for*
punishment." [50]

[48] Cited in Barclay Baron's obituary of Paterson in the *Toc H Journal*
for January 1948.
[49] *Principles of the Borstal System*, p. 12, *cf.* Osborne, *Society and Prisons,*
p. 153.
[50] *Paterson on Prisons*, p. 23, *cf.* Osborne, *op. cit.* p. 58.

Each remark was probably borrowed from the American prison reformer Thomas Mott Osborne, but they are none the worse for that. The first was used by Paterson to justify the relaxation of restraints in Borstal, the second to emphasise the point that it is the prison sentence, *i.e.*, the deprivation of liberty for a prescribed period, and not the treatment accorded in prison, that constitutes the punishment. Properly understood, this is an important half truth. It provides an answer to Du Cane's qualms about different prisoners serving the same sentence in different conditions.[51]

> " It is the length of the sentence that measures the degree of punishment and not the conditions under which it is served. A man would rather spend a week in hell than a year in an almshouse. It is therefore possible to have considerable variety in prison treatment without disregarding the basic fact that a prison sentence is still used by the courts as a form of punishment." [52]

The observation that people are sent to prison as a punishment and not for punishment is important because it serves as a warning against the ill-considered maintenance of poor prison conditions on the ground that they, in addition to the deprivation of liberty, will serve as a deterrent to the offender or to others, or that it is right that the offender should be " paid out " in this way. The observation is, however, no more than a half truth because it fails to take account of the fact that people are sentenced to imprisonment as a symbol of the community's disapproval of their conduct. Paterson was well aware of this. Before stating the aphorism he had said that a sentence of imprisonment is passed because the

[51] p. 12, *supra.*   [52] *Paterson on Prisons*, p. 23.

offender has broken the law and the court finds it necessary to express in this way its disapprobation of his conduct. " A man is not primarily sent to prison in order that he may be reformed." The fact that people are sent to prison as a punishment means that there are limits to the extent to which prison conditions can be made attractive. A prisoner who can afford them may have any number of learned periodicals sent in from outside, but, however much he is prepared to pay, he can't demand wine, women and song on the ground that he has not been sent to prison for punishment.

Paterson deserves credit for having stated as succinctly as possible the doctrines that imprisonment is a last resort and prison conditions are the concern of us all.

> " So serious—indeed, so catastrophic—is this upheaval of a free man's life that his fellows will naturally demand first that it is absolutely necessary, and if so, that it shall occur as infrequently as possible, and thirdly that the fullest examination shall be made of the conditions under which he lives in so limited and unnatural an environment." [53]

He often laid stress on the fact that what, in one of his early reports, he described as the " contraposition " of reform and punishment is largely a bogy. When speaking of Borstal, he said that the expression " a reformative penal system " challenged a comparison between the old and the new way of dealing with an offender.

> " The punishment consists more in the length of the period during which the offender is deprived of his liberty than in the conditions he is compelled to accept

[53] *Ibid.* p. 21.

during that period. He would often prefer a few months of hard labour in a prison to two years of training in a Borstal institution. It would seem therefore that punishment and reform are not antagonistic. Borstal is for the adolescent offender at once more deterrent and more reformative than prison." [54]

The extent to which it is proper to prolong incarceration in the name of reform is another question.

It is commonly said that the Criminal Justice Act 1948 is Paterson's epitaph. It abolished corporal punishment (save for offences in penal institutions), although it is not clear that Paterson was opposed to such punishment in general, and there is evidence, in the form of a minute, that he approved of it in penal institutions. The Act also contained important new provisions with regard to probation, Borstal, corrective training and preventive detention; it placed restrictions on the imprisonment of offenders under twenty-one and provided for attendance centres and detention centres as places to which such offenders can be sent. Though greatly modified by the Criminal Justice Acts of 1961 and 1967, the Act of 1948 is the basis of our present penal system.

Paterson once gave an address to the Medico-Legal Society entitled " Should the criminologist be encouraged? " The answer was in the affirmative, the conclusion distracting to a lawyer and an Oxford man:

" I suggest therefore that some public benefactor, realising that a gap remains to be filled, should found a chair at Oxford University. As it is more possible that a lawyer should understand psychology than that a psy-

[54] Introduction to *The English Borstal* by S. Barman, p. 12.

chologist should confine himself to the exactitude of law, it may be found advisable to select a lawyer for the chair." [55]

The address was given in June 1932. In view of the great achievements of Professor Radzinowicz and the Cambridge Institute of Criminology, aided and abetted in the early days by Sir Lionel Fox, it would be churlish to wish that Paterson should have had his way. I even feel constrained to doubt his conclusion with regard to the merits of a lawyer as a professor of criminology. Unless he is numerate, capable of planning and assessing research projects, familiar with the agencies of penal reform and the ways of the social scientist, a lawyer can never be more than an armchair penologist or criminologist. Apart from the salutary clarification of thought and expression which he might acquire from legal study, I cannot see what use a knowledge of law would be to a psychologist or any other kind of criminologist. I am innumerate, wholly incapable of penological research, and unfamiliar with penal agencies and the ways of the social scientist; hence the sub-title of these lectures.

5. Sir Lionel Fox

As I have already said, Sir Lionel Fox (1895–1961) became chairman of the Prison Commissioners in 1942. His main achievement in the practical sphere was the carrying out of the reforms embodied in the Criminal Justice Act 1948; but for those interested in penal reform, he will doubtless be remembered as the author of two classics, *The Modern English Prison* published in 1934 and *The English Prison*

[55] *Transactions of the Medico-Legal Society*, Vol. 26, p. 191.

and Borstal Systems published in 1952. In spite of everything that has happened since 1952, the latter remains the
most authoritative work on prisons available to the student.
It is common knowledge that Fox was also largely responsible
for the White Paper " Penal Practice in a Changing Society,"
published in 1959, which Mr. Duncan Fairn compared with
the Gladstone Report as a " considered statement of penal
policy." [56]

The period 1949–59 witnessed a great increase in the
prison population. Nonetheless, the White Paper of 1959
was able to report the following:

> " The development of an extensive system of open
> prisons; the inauguration of pre-release hostels; the
> introduction of two new forms of treatment for per-
> sistent offenders—corrective training and preventive
> detention; new types of prison with diversified func-
> tions."

The White Paper also deals with the problem of the
efficacy of imprisonment, conceding that, though it is possible
to say that such and such a percentage have not, over a given
period of exposure to risk, returned to prison, it is not
possible to say whether that result is due to their treatment
in prison, in spite of it, or whether the result would have
been the same if they had never gone to prison. The White
Paper then cites statistics published in the Report of the
Prison Commissioners for 1956 according to which " Some
87 per cent. of men and 89 per cent. of women of the Star
class [57] discharged in 1953 and 1954 had not returned to

---

[56] p. 3, *supra.*
[57] Persons aged 21 years and over who have not previously been in prison
on conviction or, if they have, are not thought likely to have a bad
influence on other prisoners.

prison under sentence by the end of 1957." These figures, it is said, "underline the crux of the prison problem, that is, the treatment of those who do come back, and especially the hard core of persistent recidivists." [58] I shall have something to say about both the figures and the problem in subsequent lectures, the point to make at this stage is that Fox, certainly more than Paterson, and possibly more than Ruggles-Brise, appreciated the importance of statistics. Paterson simply tells us that we must rely on deduction from the fundamental principles we accept rather than on induction from such figures as are presented to us.[59] He also regarded the useful science of psychology as more competent to observe than to treat. Paragraph 76 of the White Paper looks forward to the starting of work on the psychiatric prison hospital at Grendon Underwood so highly praised by last year's Hamlyn lecturer, and since said by Lord Windlesham to be "an institution regarded by many as the brightest jewel in the prison system." [60] The White Paper also recognises the value of a psychiatrically experienced doctor to prisoners who are not mentally abnormal.

Paragraph 24 of the White Paper canvassed a fundamental re-examination of penal methods, based on studies of the factors which foster or inhibit crime, and supported by a reliable assessment of the results of existing methods. The suggestion was that the examination should concern itself with the philosophy as well as the practice of punishment, and consider, not only the obligations of society and the offender to one another, but also the obligations of both to the victim. Such an examination has not taken place; its

58 Para. 48.
59 *Paterson on Prisons*, p. 28.
60 H.L. Debates, Vol. 315, col. 632 (February 17, 1971).

feasibility and desirability are the concluding topics of these lectures.

Fox deserves a special credit for having seen to it that the doings of the Prison Commission were made known to the public. He was receptive of criticism of the official approach and spoke of the Howard League for Penal Reform as " H.M.'s opposition to the Prison Commission." Times had indeed changed since 1910 when Lord Northcliffe sought to arrange for Tighe Hopkins to write a series of articles on prisons for the *London Magazine.* Ruggles-Brise rejected Tighe Hopkins on the ground that he was " a novelist and a sentimentalist." [61] He accepted instead a complacent barrister, Arthur Paterson, not to be confused, as the Webbs confused him,[62] with Alexander Paterson. The result was a pamphlet entitled " Our Prisons," a somewhat over-eulogistic account of prison life of which I have given a specimen.[63]

Fox does appear to have been a very shy man. A number of those who knew him produced a volume of commemorative essays. In one of these he is said to have " had the knack of feeling the lash that stings another's back." [64] He would certainly have endorsed a further remark contained in that essay: " Society approaches a respectable level of civilisation only when it develops an active spirit of compassion." The same sentiment was expressed fifty years earlier by Winston Churchill when speaking, on July 25, 1910, as Home Secretary in the House of Commons:

> " The mood and temper of the public in regard to the treatment of crime and criminals is one of the most

[61] Shane Leslie, *Sir Evelyn Ruggles-Brise*, p. 153.
[62] S. and B. Webb, *English Prisons Under Local Government*, p. 236, n. 1.   [63] **p.** 18, *supra.*
[64] *Studies in Penology in Memory of Sir Lionel Fox* edited by Manuel Lopez Rey and Charles Germain, p. 42.

unfailing tests of the civilisation of any country. A calm dispassionate recognition of the rights of the accused, and even of the convicted criminal, against the State—a constant heart searching by all charged with the duty of punishment—a desire and eagerness to rehabilitate in the world of industry those who have paid their due in the hard coinage of punishment: tireless efforts towards the discovery of curative and regenerative processes: unfailing faith that there is a treasure, if you can only find it, in the heart of every man. These are the symbols, which, in the treatment of crime and criminal, mark and measure the stored-up strength of a nation, and are sign and proof of the living virtue in it."

6. SUBSEQUENT DEVELOPMENTS AND OTHER AGENCIES OF PENAL REFORM

Fox was succeeded as chairman of the Prison Commission by Mr. A. W. Peterson who became head of the Prison Department of the Home Office when the Prison Commission was dissolved in 1963.

Capital punishment for murder was abolished in 1969 when the Murder (Abolition of Death Penalty) Act 1965 was continued by resolution of both Houses of Parliament. The Criminal Justice Act 1967 abolished corrective training and preventive detention, while it introduced parole and the suspended sentence. The only other statutes of penological importance passed since the days of Sir Lionel Fox are the Children and Young Persons Acts of 1963 and 1969.

In this brief description of the background of penal reform in twentieth century England, I have thought it right to concentrate on the major *dramatis personae*. I can only hope in conclusion that I will not be thought to be unaware of other institutions and persons every bit as important as those I have mentioned. Not least among these have been the Advisory Council on the Treatment of Offenders and its successor, the Advisory Council on the Penal System. Together with numerous departmental and interdepartmental committees these bodies all have, or have had, chairmen and other distinguished members who have played a major role. Then there are the pressure groups. Prominent among these is the Howard League for Penal Reform, formed in 1921 out of the Howard Association which takes us as far back as 1866, and the Penal Reform League founded in 1908. Then there are those upon whom the pressure has been exercised. There cannot be very much penal reform without Parliament and each generation has produced its crop of Members of Parliament with penological interests. Finally, there have been the successive home secretaries who have been charged with the task of getting the reforms through Parliament.

All in all, the shade of Emma Hamlyn can rest in the knowledge that there is no lack of agencies to keep England abreast, if not ahead, of other countries in the matter of penal reform.

PENAL REFORM, PUNISHMENT AND PRISON

1. THE MEANING OF PENAL REFORM

LET it be granted that there has been and still is an abundance of agencies for penal reform in twentieth century England, what can be said about their achievements? One of the purposes of these lectures is to provide an answer to this question; but I must first say something of what I mean by " penal reform." I make no secret of the fact that I find this task a surprisingly difficult one, but I do not want to spend too much time on semantics.

It is not every change in a penal system that would ordinarily be described as penal reform, even if it were thought to make for the reduction of crime. For example, if capital punishment for murder or corporal punishment for any crime were to be reintroduced into this country on account of newly discovered evidence concerning their deterrent merits, I doubt whether anyone would feel entirely at ease in describing the relevant legislation as a measure of penal reform. I would prefer to speak of the earlier legislation abolishing capital and corporal punishment as an experiment in penal reform which had failed, and the main reason for my preference would be the lack of a rehabilitative element in either form of punishment.

There is undoubtedly a close connection between the notion of penal reform and the reformatory theory of punishment. I think that any change aimed at the rehabilitation of the offender can properly be described as penal reform. This seems to be true, not only of the introduction of a new penal method, which is, like Borstal training, aimed directly at rehabilitation, but also of the introduction of rehabilitative concomitants of punishment, such as the provision of education and vocational training in prison. Furthermore, I would have no hesitation in describing as penal reform the introduction into the penal system of rehabilitative measures which are, strictly speaking, neither penal in themselves nor the concomitants of penal measures. Legislation, providing for the possibility of hospital orders for mentally abnormal offenders, or for care orders in the case of delinquent children, comes into this category. Such orders result in treatment as opposed to punishment, although the fact that they may be as coercive as prison sentences means that the distinction between treatment and punishment is far from clear cut.

What should be said of the introduction of a non-punitive measure which is neither therapeutic nor corrective? For example, was the introduction of the double-track system of preventive detention by the Prevention of Crime Act 1908 penal reform? Under that Act a habitual criminal might be sentenced to a period of preventive detention to follow upon the sentence of penal servitude imposed for his last offence. The period of preventive detention was not intended to be punitive; the protection of the public was its aim, and the sentence was meant to be served in conditions far superior to those of penal servitude. The scheme did not work well in practice, at any rate in its later days, but I think that its introduction can properly be described as penal reform. The Act recognised that even a habitual criminal must not be punished excessively for his latest offence, although it might be necessary to isolate him as humanely as was reasonably possible from the rest of society for a considerable time.

At the other end of the scale from preventive detention come absolute or conditional discharges, and suspended prison sentences. They have little to do with either rehabilitation or the protection of society, but I would nonetheless regard legislation providing for them as a measure of penal reform on account of the humanitarianism of its motive. The suffering caused by punishment is either not to be inflicted at all, or else to be conditionally suspended.

I suggest therefore that the notion of penal reform should be extended so as to allow for the inclusion of measures, the primary aim of which is humanitarian, *i.e.* the provision of whatever control of crime the penal system can achieve with the minimum of suffering to the offender and those connected with him. I would like to take this opportunity of protesting against the tendency to belittle humanitarianism as a yardstick of progress in penal matters, notwithstanding the clarity with which it was recognised as such a yardstick by Churchill and others quoted in my first lecture. The tendency is not only discernible in the " hangers and floggers "; I have noticed it in many an advocate of penal reform. For example, it is all too common for people to understress the argument that probation is preferable to imprisonment because it is more humane, and to overstress the argument that probation is not a soft option on account of the magnitude of the demands made on the probationer. Similarly, in the course of the argument about capital punishment, there were weak kneed abolitionists who conceded that, if convinced that one hanging a year would prevent one extra murder a year, they would at once become retentionists. Of course the humanitarian argument has to be weighed against arguments based on deterrence, but an abolitionist worth his salt would stick to his guns a little longer than the abolitionists I have mentioned. He would say that capital punishment is an institution so grossly inhumane that it is plainly not justified if it deters no more potential murderers in a given year than the number of past murderers hanged during that year. I conclude that a change in the penal system can properly be described as an endeavour to achieve penal reform if it is aimed directly or indirectly at the rehabilitation of the offender, or if its object is to avoid, suspend or reduce punishment on humanitarian grounds. From time to time there will inevitably be tension between the objectives of penal reform and the commonly accepted aims of punishment. It is legitimate to raise the question whether there has been too much or too little penal reform in the twentieth century and I do this in my final lecture.

But does it make sense to speak, as I have spoken, of a reformatory theory of punishment? Is it a justification of the practice of punishing that it may have an improving effect on the offender? In the context of these lectures, " punishment " means the infliction of pain by the State on someone convicted of an offence, and it will generally be convenient to have a fairly serious offence in mind, with imprisonment as the typical example of the pain. Obviously it makes sense to speak of individual deterrence as opposed to reform, and to say that the State properly punishes a convicted thief in the hope that the fear of further punishment will stop him from offending again. Retribution and general deterrence are likewise comprehensible justifications of punishment, however wrong-headed some of us may consider some forms of the former to be, and however sceptical others may be about the latter; but many people would say that it does not make sense to speak of the State punishing an offender in order that he may become genuinely penitent and perceive the moral error of his ways. There is force in the following words of Bernard Shaw: " If you are to punish a man retributively, you must injure him. If you are to reform him you must improve him. And men are not improved by injuries." [1]

2. EWING'S EDUCATIVE THEORY OF PUNISHMENT

I shall give the answer to the question whether the reformatory theory of punishment makes sense in the words of Dr. A. C. Ewing, Fellow of Jesus College, Cambridge, who was, until recently, Reader in Moral Philosophy in the University of Cambridge. His *Morality of Punishment*, published in 1929, has claims to be regarded as the most original full-scale contribution to the philosophy of punishment published in England during this century. It is of especial interest to those concerned with the theoretical aspects of penal reform on account of the author's obvious familiarity with contemporary prison practice. The book is also of especial interest to English lawyers because some of the views expressed in it are a refined twentieth century version of the robust, though repulsively expressed, views of Sir James Fitzjames Stephen (1829–94), a Queen's Bench Judge and the great nineteenth century expositor of our criminal law. Moreover, Ewing's views on the educative effects of punishment on the community are akin to those of some contemporary English judges who attach importance to the denunciatory element in punishment. But first let me show how he justifies punish-

---

[1] Preface to S. and B. Webb, *English Prisons Under Local Government*, p. xiv.

ment on account of its possible reformative effect on the
offender.

Education of the offender.   Ewing describes his theory
as " educative " and I think that its pith can be gathered from
the following passage:

> " Usually the offender is himself conscious that he has
> been acting wrongly, and for him to be reformed this
> consciousness must become predominant.   (By this is
> meant not a morbid dwelling on past sins, but simply the
> recognition by the agent that his act must not be
> repeated.)   Anything that emphasises his guilt will tend,
> other things being equal, in this direction; and no more
> striking emphasis can be given to his guilt than by public
> condemnation and punishment.   It is here, if anywhere,
> that we may find the moral, educative function of punish-
> ment *qua* punishment both in regard to the offender and
> in regard to others.   Punishment may reform by rendering
> possible the application of other educative influences, it
> may reform by deterring through the sheer painfulness
> of it; but if it is to produce a moral effect as punishment,
> not merely as a preventive safeguard, a convenient means
> of securing a compulsory training or a natural pain, it
> must reform by calling attention to the badness of the act.
> Pain that merely happens to follow wrongdoing does not
> impress on the offender's mind that his act was bad;
> pain inflicted deliberately for wrongdoing after a con-
> sidered judgment by an impartial authority is much more
> likely to do so." [2]

[2] A. C. Ewing, *The Morality of Punishment*, p. 84.   The words in
brackets are Ewing's footnote.

In short, the answer to Bernard Shaw is that the actual experience of the pain of punishment may reform the offender on account of its cathartic effect. To put the same point in more homely terms, it may awaken a " serve me right " feeling.[3] The number of offenders permanently affected in this way in contemporary Britain is, in all probability, extremely small; but the actual or even the potential existence of one such offender is sufficient to refute the suggestion that the reformatory theory of punishment does not make theoretical sense. All the same, the probable paucity of persons likely to be reformed by punishment *qua* punishment means that the practice of punishment cannot be justified on the reformatory ground alone, for the evils attendant on the punishment of the unreformed, such as their own suffering, the suffering of their families, and the cost to the State, would greatly exceed the benefits flowing from the rare reformations.

It is important to pay heed to Ewing's distinction between punishment which may reform by the cathartic process whereby the offender is brought to see the moral error of his ways, punishment which merely deters and punishment which is accompanied by the possibility of some independent educative process. To be deterred by fear of a repetition of the punishment, though a great deal better than remaining undeterred, is not to be reformed. Punishment which renders possible the application of reformative influences such as the ministrations of the chaplain or the inculcation of regular work habits in prison, is not reformative as such although it is the possibility of bringing these influences to bear which most people have in mind when they speak of the reformatory theory of punishment. The extent to which the possibility

[3] Lord Haldane, cited in Kenny's *Outlines of Criminal Law* (15th ed.), p. 33.

of reformation can ever justify the prolongation of a deprivation of liberty for a period greater than that thought to be
justified on deterrent or retributive grounds is considered at
subsequent points in these lectures.

Education of the community.   Ewing stresses the fact
that the punishment of an offender may have an educative
effect on others.   Elsewhere I have called this a theory of
" long term " deterrence as distinct from the short term
deterrence based solely on the tendency of the example of
punishment to deter those contemplating conduct similar to
that of the offender; but " educative " may well be thought
to be a better word.[4]

To quote Ewing:

" But surely this solemn, public condemnation on behalf
of the community will have some effect not only on those
actually punished but on others also.   If it may help the
offender to realise the badness of his action, may it not
help others to realise this badness before they have committed the kind of action in question at all?   This must
not be confused with the purely deterrent effect.   A man
who abstains from crime just because he is deterred
abstains through fear of suffering and not because he
thinks it wicked; a man who abstains because the condemnation of the crime by society and the State has
brought its wickedness home to him abstains from moral
motives and not merely from fear of unpleasant consequences to himself." [5]

4 *The English Sentencing System*, p. 108.
5 Ewing, *op. cit.* p. 94.

Just as Ewing supplements the notion of deterrence of the actual offender through fear of a repetition of the punishment with the notion of reform through catharsis, he supplements the notion of the deterrence of potential offenders by threat or example with the notion of education by denunciation of anti-social conduct. It has been doubted whether people can be said to be morally improved if they come to regard an action as morally worse *solely* because it is made punishable by law.[6] But Ewing's point is a negative one, we would all be in danger of moral deterioration if morally bad acts now punishable by law were *consistently* to go unpunished.

> "When a law is broken the governing body cannot sit still and do nothing for such inaction would definitely encourage and in a sense even sanction other crimes. So it is easy to see that the neglect to punish will have consequences which are morally harmful. It will tend to make some people think that lawlessness does not matter, it will render the laws and government despicable in the eyes of many, and the moral judgments of those who represent and rule the State, being not carried out in action, will cease to be taken seriously at all." [7]

In short, one reason why we punish morally bad actions is in order to maintain our moral standards. I said that Ewing's point is that we would all be in danger of moral deterioration if acts punishable by law were to go unpunished *consistently* because the theory only demands a regular, not an invariable, practice of punishing convicted criminals. The theory is not antipathetic to probation, binding over or discharges.

[6] C. W. K. Mundle in *The Philosophy of Punishment* (ed. H. B. Acton), p. 67.

[7] Ewing, *op. cit.* p. 95.

Stephen. In this respect Ewing's version of the educative theory of punishment can be regarded as an advance on that of Stephen; but this is not the point that I want to stress. Stephen said:

> " Great part of the general detestation of crime which happily prevails amongst the decent part of the community in all civilised countries arises from the fact that the commission of offences is associated in all such communities with the solemn and deliberate infliction of punishment *wherever* crime is proved." [8]

I do not stress the point because it would be improper to attach too much to the word " wherever " and, in any event, having regard to the time when he used the word (1883) Stephen can hardly be supposed to have had the possibility of refraining from punishing convicted offenders in the forefront of his mind. The point that I do want to stress is the greater refinement of Ewing's theory.

Stephen's version of the educative theory was the outcome of a crudely retributive theory of punishment, *viz.* that a justification of punishment is the satisfaction which it affords to the desire for vengeance on the criminal experienced by his victim and many other people.

> " I think it highly desirable that criminals should be hated, that the punishments inflicted upon them should be so contrived as to give expression to that hatred, and to justify it, so far as the public provision of means for expressing and gratifying a natural healthy sentiment can justify and encourage it." [9]

[8] *History of Criminal Law*, Vol. 2, p. 80. Italics supplied.
[9] *Op. cit.* p. 82.

For good measure, Stephen went on to advocate " the increased use of physical pain by flogging or *otherwise*, by way of secondary punishment," [10] together with an increase in the severity of flogging.   " At present it is little, if at all, more serious than a birching at a public school."

Ewing, by contrast, would have the public resentment concentrated on the crime rather than on the criminal; he considers that we should regard the sufferings of the guilty as something to be reduced to the lowest dimensions compatible with the interests of society; and he concludes that the ideal, on his theory, would be for the punishment to consist only in moral condemnation.   He recognises, however, that a penalty additional to the moral condemnation has to be imposed, partly for deterrent reasons, partly because neither the offender nor the community would feel that the government was taking the matter seriously if it proceeded by censure alone.

Those who consider punishment to be a dirty word can go a long way towards justifying their views by pointing to Stephen, and the greatest credit is due to Ewing for having expounded a theory of punishment so similar to Stephen's in its application to persons other than the offender, and so much more civilised than Stephen's in its application to the offender.

Ewing expressly rejects that form of the retributive theory of punishment according to which the justification of punishment is the return of suffering for moral evil voluntarily done. He would have no truck with that form of the retributive theory according to which the justification of punishment is the gratification of the desire for vengeance of the victim of

[10] *Op. cit.* p. 91.   Italics supplied.

the crime and those connected with him. He does not think that " retributive " is the right word for his own educative theory, but he is by no means oblivious of what are commonly called " retributive " elements in the practice of punishment.

Hart. It has, however, been left to Professor Hart to sort out the different contexts in which a view about punishment can be said to be " retributive " and to show that, even if we justify the general practice of punishment on deterrent grounds, the claims of deterrence must be qualified by retributive considerations such as the necessity of apportioning the amount of punishment with the deserts of the offender and the gravity of his offence. Hart's main contention is that, in the case of punishment, as in that of many other social institutions, the pursuit of one aim may be qualified by, or provide an opportunity for, the pursuit of another; surely the following is the most telling remark of the century on the philosophy of punishment:

> " Till we have developed this sense of the complexity of punishment . . . we shall be in no fit state to assess the extent to which the whole institution has been eroded by or needs to be adapted to new beliefs about the human mind." [11]

Throughout this and the following lecture I shall assume that the whole institution has not yet been eroded, but I will return to the thoughts provoked by Professor Hart's remark in my fourth lecture.

[11] *Punishment and Responsibility*, p. 3.

Priorities. Both Stephen and Ewing accept the ordinary utilitarian aims of punishment based on deterrence and incapacitation. Once it is accepted that punishment can have more than one object, questions of priority are apt to arise. Two sharply contrasted solutions of especial relevance to reform in prison have been propounded.

Writing in 1883 Sir Edward Fry, a Lord Justice of Appeal, said:

> "As each reason for punishment is independent and sufficient, it follows that the greatest punishment justified by any one independent reason ought to be inflicted. If A, B, C and D be punishments in an ascending scale, and if, having regard only to the malignity of the offence, I should inflict A; if I regard the reformation of the culprit B, if I regard the prevention of further offences by the culprit C, and if I regard the repression of offences in others D, I ought, so I think, to inflict the last and greatest punishment; for the repression of offences in others is a legitimate aim and end of society, and the culprit has no merits which he can oppose to his thus being made useful for the good of society." [12]

The implication is that, if the requirements of deterrence and retribution could be met by six months' imprisonment, while a year was necessary for reform, a year's imprisonment would be the proper sentence for the judge to impose.

Professor Norval Morris of Chicago, one of the leading criminologists of our time, has said:

> "Power over a criminal's life should not be taken in excess of that which would be taken were his reform not

[12] *Nineteenth Century*, Vol. 14, p. 526.

considered as one of our purposes. The maximum of his punishment should never be greater than that which would be justified by the other aims of our criminal justice. Under the lower ceiling of that sentence, we should utilise our reformative skills to a system towards social readjustment; but we should never seek to justify an extension of power over him on the ground that we may thus more likely effect his reform." [13]

This would mean that six months would be the proper sentence in the case I have put.

The sharpness of the contrast is robbed of much of its practical significance by the fact that no one has more than the most rudimentary idea of the term of imprisonment appropriate in a given case to the demands of deterrence, retribution or reform; but the contrast is of importance in relation to short prison sentences which, by common consent, give no opportunity for the exercise of such reformative influences as prison can provide, and in relation to Borstal training. These matters are mentioned in my next lecture.

3. CAPITAL AND CORPORAL PUNISHMENT

Prison conditions are to be the major theme of the rest of this lecture, but the total abolition of corporal punishment and the practical abolition of capital punishment must be given pride of place in any account of penal reform in twentieth century England, however brief may be the manner in which it is proposed to deal with them. They have much in common. The retention of each of these measures for so long illustrates what I can only describe, with apologies to the shade of

[13] *Chicago Law Review*, Vol. 33, p. 638.

Emma Hamlyn, as the English atavistic attachment to barbarous methods of punishment; and the abolition of each was probably disapproved by the majority of the public, just as it was opposed for a long time by the majority of Queen's Bench judges. In each instance too, there is room for a sophisticated argument that the abolition was not penal reform because it was inhumane. I need hardly say that I do not accept the argument in either case, but I think it is worth mentioning.

Capital punishment. So far as capital punishment is concerned, the argument derives support from Sir Alexander Paterson's memorandum submitted to the select committee of 1930 which ultimately recommended abolition for an experimental period of five years.

> " I gravely doubt whether an average man can serve more than ten continuous years in prison without deterioration. If so slight an alternative to the death sentence is considered to be lacking in deterrence, and terms of 20 years are inevitable, then the choice is between a penalty that destroys the personal life and one that will, in the vast majority of cases, permanently impair something more precious than the life of the physical body." [14]

The doubt was based on first hand acquaintance with men who are undergoing protracted terms of imprisonment as an alternative to the death penalty. As one who is totally lacking in practical knowledge of the effects of long terms

[14] *Paterson on Prisons*, p. 143. The text is based on my essay in *The Hanging Question*, published by the Howard League for Penal Reform in 1969, and edited by Professor Blom Cooper, Q.C.

of imprisonment, I use the " times have changed " reply with considerable diffidence. Nonetheless, the retentionists' case based on the cruelty of alternatives to capital punishment probably had been weakened by improvements in prison conditions by the time the Murder (Abolition of Death Penalty) Act 1965 was passed. Moreover, the period during which a life prisoner is detained in custody is generally less than it was in Paterson's day. It is less than " the period which varies from fifteen to twenty years in a convict prison " said by him to have been served in his day by those who just escaped the scaffold. At any rate the " times have changed " reply was accepted by the chairman of the Royal Commission on Capital Punishment which sat from 1949 to 1953.[15]

I shall have something to say about long prison sentences in my next lecture, but it is appropriate at this stage to stress the qualified nature of Paterson's doubt. It was confined to terms of imprisonment of ten continuous years.

> " Until a sentence of ten years is considered an adequate substitute for capital punishment, I will prefer the death sentence, on the grounds of humanity, to any alternative that any country has tried."

Is it beyond the bounds of reasonable possibility that we shall live to see the day when ten continuous years is recognised as the maximum permissible period of incarceration for anyone who is neither mentally ill nor believed by the prison authorities to be someone who would constitute a really serious danger to the public if he were released?

The story of the abolition of capital punishment for murder need only be told in the barest outline. The recommendation of the select committee of 1930 was not accepted

---

[15] Gowers, *A Life for a Life*, p. 129,

immediately; but a clause abolishing capital punishment for murder for an experimental period of five years was inserted in the Criminal Justice Bill 1948. It found favour with the Commons but was rejected by the House of Lords. There followed the Royal Commission of 1949–53. Its terms of reference, confined as they were to the limitation as opposed to the abolition of capital punishment, rendered it a *tour de force*, but the excellence of the body of its report more than made amends. The Commons again voted in favour of abolition in 1956, but the only result was the restriction of capital punishment to the types of murder specified in the Homicide Act 1957 (murder in the course of theft, murder of a police or prison officer in the execution of his duty, murder by shooting or causing an explosion, and second or subsequent murders). The Murder (Abolition of Death Penalty) Act 1965 made the punishment for all murders imprisonment for life; but the life sentence for murder is different from other life sentences because the court may declare the minimum period which in its view should elapse before the Home Secretary orders the offender's release on licence. The Act was of temporary duration in the first instance, but it was made permanent by resolution of both Houses of Parliament in 1969.

These developments have left two questions behind them, and each is currently under consideration by the Criminal Law Revision Committee. The first concerns the definition of murder. Is it necessary, for example, to preserve the distinction between murder and manslaughter? And, if so, should that distinction retain its present form in view of the fact that it largely stems from the existence of capital punishment for murder? The second question concerns the sentence for murder. Should the judge have power to dictate rather than recommend the minimum period of incarceration? Should there be a mandatory fixed term sentence? Or should life simply be a maximum, as in the case of manslaughter?

Capital punishment is still possible in the cases of treason and piracy, hence my previous allusion to practical as opposed to total abolition.

Corporal punishment. The argument that the abolition of judicial corporal punishment by the Criminal Justice Act 1948 was not penal reform because it was inhumane is even more sophisticated than that which concerns the supposed inhumanity of the abolition of capital punishment. The argument is that, if the courts had power to order corporal punishment, they could, by exercising that power in appropriate cases, either spare the offender a custodial sentence altogether, or else give him a short one, thereby avoiding or diminishing the disruption of his life. I do not think this argument will bear scrutiny, even if one is prepared to accept the birching of a child by a stranger long after the offence as a permissible form of punishment. Much depends on the offender's age group. For boys under fourteen, corporal punishment only seems to be appropriate for the less serious offences for which no court would contemplate removal from a satisfactory home background. In any event, when the Children and Young Persons Act 1969 is fully in force, criminal proceedings for offences other than homicide will be impossible, and a birching is hardly suitable as the sole punishment for homicide. In the case of a boy between the ages of fourteen and seventeen, corporal punishment might occasionally be a suitable alternative to a detention centre, but there is the well-nigh insuperable problem of choosing the right boy. If psychology tells us anything, it is that this is a very real problem. In any event a detention centre order will not be possible for a boy in this age group when the Act of 1969 is fully operative, and criminal proceedings against such boys will be restricted. The only order likely to be disruptive of the offender's life would be a care order and such an order will only be made in practice where the home background is unsatisfactory. In the case of offenders over seventeen, corporal punishment only seems to be appropriate, if appropriate at all, for offences which are so serious that it would only be possible for it to be the sole punishment in the most exceptional circumstances; however short the accompanying custodial sentence might be, its imposition would be regarded, not without reason, as double punishment. Judicial corporal punishment was abolished in consequence of the report of the Cadogan Committee published in 1938. That report contains salutary statements of fact which are all too often forgotten. It is not the case that no one has ever been flogged twice; it is not the case that the subsequent records of criminals who had been flogged were better, in comparable instances, than those of criminals who had not been flogged; it is not the case that convictions for robbery with violence in Liverpool declined after Day J.'s actions, involving corporal punishment, against the " high rip " gang in the 1880s. The report also contains the following statement calculated to bring a blush to the cheek of every self-respecting Englishman.

" It may be said that, as a penalty for criminal offences by adults, corporal punishment has been abandoned by every civilised country in the world except those—*i.e.* the British Dominions and, to a very limited extent, the United States of America—in which the development of the criminal code has been influenced largely by the English criminal law." [16]

Even so, there was great pressure for the reintroduction of corporal punishment in 1959, and the greatest credit is due to the Advisory Council on the Treatment of Offenders for having resisted it in a report published in 1960. The United Kingdom representative in several of the foreign countries in which further enquiry was made by the Council reported that it was unthinkable that there should be any return to corporal punishment in those countries, and that comment there on the current demand in this country was severely critical.[17]

4. PRISON CONDITIONS

For the rest of this lecture I want to consider the extent to which prison conditions have improved since 1895 and the extent to which they are conducive to reform.

A day in a prisoner's life. Let me begin with an account of a day in the life of a prisoner over twenty-one under sentence in Oxford Prison in 1971. He will be roused by a bell, or the full blast of the prison radio, at 6.30 a.m. He will then get up, wash at the wash-hand-stand in his cell, dress in his prison clothes (his ordinary clothes having been taken away from him together with the rest of his property on reception into prison) and clean his cell.

At 7 o'clock his cell will be unlocked by his landing officer. The prisoner will then proceed, together with other prisoners, under the supervision of the officer to carry his chamber pot to a recess on the landing where he will go through the notoriously revolting task of " slopping out."

[16] Cmd. 5684, para. 38.   [17] Cmd. 1213, para. 40.

He and the other prisoners may well have been in their cells for the past twelve hours without any practical possibility of being let out in order to attend to the necessities of nature.

Having replaced his chamber pot in his cell, the prisoner may fetch hot water from the recess in a plastic jug from his wash-hand-stand. At 7.20 he will queue for breakfast at a service point in the ground floor hall. He will bring his breakfast back to his cell on a steel tray with sunken compartments. He is then locked in his cell by the landing officer who hands him a razor blade. He eats his breakfast and shaves. The breakfast should be both satisfying and satisfactory. On April 15, 1971, the menu was tea, bread, margarine, porridge, sugar and boiled egg.

At about 7.50 the cell is unlocked, the prisoner returns his razor blade to his landing officer and is escorted to his work together with other prisoners by another officer. The work done in the prison workshops is mainly the manufacture of tents and sleeping bags under contract with outside firms, and the assembly of components of various kinds such as valves for aerosol sprays. The proverbial mailbag sewing still goes on, but principally as a makeshift when other work is not available. Allowance must also be made for a number of prisoners who work in the kitchen, laundry, garden or maintenance department. On the whole the tempo of work is leisurely, were it otherwise there would not be enough work to go round.

At 11.15 the prisoner is escorted by an officer together with other prisoners from the workshop, in which we will assume that he has been working, to the exercise yard. He walks around the yard, talking to other prisoners, and smoking if he is so minded and has tobacco; but all the time under the supervision of an officer. At 11.45 he is taken back to his cell with other prisoners. At midday he queues for lunch which he brings back to his cell in which he is locked until 1.30. The meal is well served, and there is a choice of dishes. On April 15 the menu was soup, roll, meat pasty or faggot and gravy, or Irish stew, mashed potato, cabbage, gravy, jam tart, custard and a pint of tea. At 1.30 the cell is unlocked and the prisoners are escorted to the exercise ground for half an hour's more walking. From 2.10 to 4.50 they are back at work, and at 5.00 they queue for tea. On April 15 the menu was tea, bread, margarine, pork luncheon meat and chipped potatoes. Tea is eaten in the cell, and the prisoner may well stay there until 7 o'clock the next morning, except that he will be let out for a brief moment between 6 and 7 p.m. in order to relieve himself, replenish the water in his cell, and do any necessary slopping out. At 7 o'clock tea will be brought to his cell by an orderly and the prisoner may eat with it the supper food which he will have brought with him with his previous meal. On April 15 this consisted of a dripping roll. Lights go out about 8.30.

It is necessary to mention certain further matters in order to complete the picture of our prisoner's life. He may receive one visit of half an hour's duration each month from not more than three people named by him; he may write one letter a week at the expense of the State, and two more if he pays for them. He may be kept in contact with his family through the good offices of the prison welfare officer who will discuss the post-release prospects with him. He may have as many books as he likes from the prison library and others will be procured for him if he so desires; he may also have a newspaper sent in from outside if he pays for it. The wherewithal to provide for these additional comforts come from his prison earnings which are unlikely to exceed 35p a week. They may also be devoted to the purchase of tobacco, and other small luxuries, from the prison canteen which is open at exercise time twice a week. Our prisoner may also make complaints to the governor, have interviews with the chaplain and receive weekly visits from a prison visitor. Prison visitors are volunteers from outside appointed annually by the prison department. They visit the prisoner in his cell, and converse with him about general topics. The prisoner is asked whether he wishes to have such visits when he is received into prison. All bathing in Oxford prison takes place between 6 and 8 p.m. There is thus a further opportunity for a prisoner to be out of his cell for a short while on one evening a week. Moreover, if our prisoner attends any one or more of a fairly large number of evening classes, he will be out of his cell between 6 and 8 on the relevant evenings. The fact remains that he may have to spend as much as sixteen out of the twenty-four hours in a cell of 13 by 7 feet. Worse still, according to most people's standards of privacy, the cell may have two other occupants. Even more time may be spent in the cell over weekends, although every prisoner is let out for periods during which he may watch television and associate with other prisoners. I have assumed that our prisoner is over twenty-one because young prisoners under twenty-one lead a more active life in association in a separate wing. A very limited number of fortunate adults eat their meals and spend their leisure time out of their cells in association with other prisoners at Oxford.

I have selected Oxford prison as the basis of my account of a day in a prisoner's life because it is my " local " with a governor and staff who coped with my pettifogging questions with the patience of Job. But the choice has incidental advantages. Although the inmates look upon it as a " friendly nick," Oxford occupies a lowly place on the Home Office prison class list. Of course this is in no sense due to any fault on the part of the governor or staff. The low grading of Oxford and all other local prisons is due to the utter impossibility of utilising prison buildings designed for a comparatively small number of inmates serving their sentences under the separate system, to house a much greater number under a system which aims at allowing prisoners as much time out of their cells as possible. Oxford prison will soon be closed, but its low ranking in the class list does serve to sharpen the contrast between a closed local prison and an open prison, and between the conditions of today and those which prevailed at the time of the Gladstone Report.

Local and open prisons. A local prison is one to which prisoners are taken immediately after they have been sentenced, but it also has to cope with prisoners on remand. This means that, instead of attending to prisoners under sentence, the staff may be required to escort remand prisoners to and from court, to be in sight, though out of hearing, at interviews had by such prisoners with their legal advisers, and to assist in the preparation of numerous reports for the courts. Except in the case of those serving very short sentences, local prisons should be no more than allocation centres for prisoners under sentence, but this is very far from being the case at present.

Open prisons are said to be " held universally and rightly as the great humane twentieth century contribution to rehabilitation." [18] So far as England is concerned, the idea is

[18] Klare, *The Anatomy of Prison*, p. 120.

said to have come to Sir Alexander Paterson when, following a visit to an open prison in the United States, he was driven a considerable distance to a railway station by a convicted driver who was to return to prison alone after Paterson had caught his train.

Open prisons are often converted private houses or army hospitals in large grounds. As might have been anticipated, conditions are far easier and freer than those in a local prison. This may be illustrated by a brief comparison with the life at Oxford prison. The inmates sleep in unlocked dormitories or cubicles and there is no slopping out problem. All meals are taken in the communal dining room. The inmates go to their allocated work at the appointed time unescorted. There are periodical " tallies " or checks to ascertain that all the prisoners are there, but inmates are otherwise free to move about the premises and grounds as they like. Accordingly there is no regular exercise period. After the evening meal until lights out, that is from about 5.30 to 9.00, the inmates may read, play cards or chess, watch television or talk as they please.

It is said that about 20 per cent. of convicted prisoners can reasonably be trusted in open conditions. They constitute category D—the lowest security risk; but they do not by any means all find their way to open prisons. This is partly because the government often has to allay the understandable apprehensions of the local population by undertaking not to place certain offenders, *e.g.* those guilty of violent crimes or sex offences against children, in a particular open prison.[19] It it not uncommon for prisoners serving long sentences to be transferred to an open prison as the day of

[19] *People in Prison*, para. 169.

their release approaches. A number of non-violent offenders, such as fraudulent solicitors or accountants, may well spend most of their sentence in one of these prisons.

Training prisons. In addition to local and open prisons, there are numerous closed training prisons. Conditions in these institutions vary considerably. In some medium security training prisons, the inmates sleep in dormitories or cubicles as in an open prison; in other cellular maximum security prisons, there is a far more active industrial regime and more vocational training than there is in an open prison. Life in one of the large London or provincial prisons is inevitably very different for better and for worse, from that in a small " friendly nick " like Oxford; it is impossible for the staff to know the inmates as well. Attached to some prisons are pre-release hostels from which the inmates go out to regular daily work in the community, returning to their hostel each night. Their earnings are used for their maintenance, and the maintenance of their families and for their own pocket money, the balance being saved. Further details about life in the widely varying training prisons are unnecessary for the purpose of contrasting conditions with those which prevailed at the time of the Gladstone Report and for a considerable time after its publication.

Contrast with the past. How far have prison conditions improved since 1895? The answer to this question is that prison is undoubtedly a much more comfortable place than it was, apart from the slopping out and the overcrowding, two matters which are of course closely related to each other.

Some very chastening reading with regard to overcrowding is to be found in the repealed section 17 (1) of the Prison Act

1865 and regulation 26 in the first schedule to that Act. Section 17 (1) read

> " In every prison separate cells shall be provided equal in number to the average of the greatest number of prisoners, not being convicts under sentence of penal servitude, who have been confined in such prisons at the same time during each preceding 5 years."

Regulation 26 provided that every male prisoner should sleep in a cell by himself, or, under special circumstances, in a separate bed placed in a cell containing not fewer than two other male prisoners.

The first head of the Gladstone Committee's terms of reference concerned the accommodation provided for prisoners and the operation of section 17 (1) together with regulation 26. Serious charges of overcrowding in London prisons had been made. What had been happening was that increasing numbers of prisoners sentenced to penal servitude had been drafted to local prisons for the first part of their sentence, the part which had to be served in solitary confinement, instead of spending it in a convict prison. The result was that, owing to the exclusion of convicts serving sentences of penal servitude from its provisions, section 17 (1) had failed to ensure that there was invariably separate cell accommodation for all those received into local prisons under sentence of imprisonment. The committee deplored the practice of sending convicts sentenced to penal servitude to local prisons,[20] and recommended that the transfer of prisoners from one prison to another be made easier. They were also critical of the phrase " special circumstances " in regulation 26: " We think that association in sleeping cells should not

[20] Report of the Interdepartmental Committee on Prisons (1895), para. 80.

be allowed under any circumstances except for medical reasons and upon the express recommendation of the medical officer." [21]   That was the end of overcrowding of prisons in England until some time after the second world war. Now that the daily average number of persons in custody in prison service establishments [22] exceeds 40,000 with some 14,000 sleeping two or three to a cell, the following provisions of section 14 of the Prison Act 1952 have a somewhat hollow ring:

" 1. The Secretary of State shall satisfy himself from time to time that in every prison sufficient accommodation is provided for all prisoners."

" 2. No cell shall be used for the confinement of a prisoner unless it is certified by an inspector that its size, lighting, heating, ventilation and fittings are adequate for health and that it allows the prisoner to communicate at any time with a prison officer."

It is possible for a prisoner to summon a member of the night patrol to his cell by ringing a bell, but action will only be taken in an extreme emergency, certainly not on account of the calls of nature.

It is pleasant to learn that all new prisons are being designed to avoid the need for slopping out, and that experiments in the automatic unlocking of cells may provide the means of solving the problem of night sanitation in existing prisons, but it is certainly depressing to be told that there is no early prospect of getting rid of slopping out in most of our closed prisons. [23]

In order to appreciate the improvements, it is necessary

---

[21] *Ibid.* para. 31.
[22] Prisons, Borstals and detention centres.
[23] *People in Prison*, para. 185.

to remember that, in 1895, the current philosophy was that of " hard labour, hard fare and a hard bed."

So far as the labour was concerned, if the sentence were one of imprisonment with hard labour, it might take the form of a treadmill or crank; even when the sentence was one of simple imprisonment, the cellular labour would as like as not be oakum picking, the teasing out of tarred rope for caulking the seams of ships, with its attendant agony to the fingers and the accompanying threat of the withholding of some of the already scanty rations if so many pounds of rope were not teased out during the day.[24] A cynic might say that the stripping of old telephone wires by the modern prisoner is merely a variant of oakum picking, but an instrument is provided; this could have happened in the case of the oakum, but the instrument does not appear to have been altogether adequate to alleviate the strain on the fingers. Moreover, the stripping of so many wires is not a condition precedent to the next meal.

As to the fare, all that need be said is that, in 1901, and for a considerable time thereafter, a prisoner got 8 ounces of bread and a pint of gruel for breakfast every day. This was the effect of the " improved " dietary rules introduced in 1901. The daily dose for supper (the equivalent of tea in Oxford prison today) was 8 ounces of bread and a pint of porridge; variety at dinner from day to day was minimal. All the prison menus of 1971 vary from day to day. On April 16 there was tomato and fried bacon for breakfast at Oxford prison instead of the boiled egg of April 15.

In 1895 the prisoner's bed would, in all probability, have

---

[24] Anon., *Five Years Penal Servitude* (1879), p. 44. In what follows I have made use of this book by an ex-convict, and *I was in Prison* by Brocklehurst (1898), an account of life in Strangeways prison.

been a mere plank during the first month of his sentence. This meant that the oakum became a blessing in disguise for it could be made to serve as a kind of mattress or pillow, although its use for such purposes was frowned upon.[25] It is true that Mr. Bernard Faulk, a journalist who served a four-day sentence for contempt of court in Crumlin Road Prison, Belfast, in 1971, says that the beds and pillows were as hard as planks,[26] but at least he was using a metaphor. The survival of the plank bed for the first fortnight of a sentence of imprisonment with hard labour until 1945 is one of the proofs of the tenacity of the belief that prison conditions must be made to act as a deterrent by means of petty inhumanities in spite of the acceptance of the view that the deterrent is the loss of liberty and disgrace which imprisonment entails. This view, repeatedly asserted by Sir Alexander Paterson and Sir Lionel Fox, was current in official circles at least as early as 1911, as is shown by the following extract from a report to the Secretary of State for Scotland on the Washington Penitentiary Congress of 1910.

> " Unless for very short periods, it is not in fact in civilised countries now possible, even if thought desirable, to impose such conditions and hardship as would themselves act as deterrents. Loss of liberty is the real deterrent, combined with the feeling of disgrace which the more sensitive experience." [27]

It is also necessary, in order to appreciate the improvement in prison conditions since 1895, to remember that, when the Gladstone Report was published, the separate system prevailed in local prisons and during the first nine months

[25] Brocklehurst, *op. cit.* pp. 30–31; p. 69.
[26] *The Listener*, May 11, 1971.   [27] Cmd. 5640, paras. 19–20.

of a sentence of penal servitude. Even when penal servitude convicts worked in association, a strict rule of silence prevailed. One of the most striking condemnations of the separate system is to be found, to my mind, in the fact that, in the days when each cell was provided with a primitive w.c. some prisoners were wont to empty the bowl and use the refuse pipe as a speaking tube to the seven other cells on the same drain.[28] If it had not been necessary to abandon the cellular w.c.s on account of the inadequacy of the plumbing arrangements, it might, ironically enough, have been necessary to do so in order to remove unhygienic temptations. " The last vestiges of the rule of silence have long since disappeared in the noise of radios in workshops, and people in custody may now talk freely to each other." [29] Its retention, albeit in an increasingly attenuated form, far into the twentieth century is eloquent testimony to the persistence with which mankind sometimes endeavours to achieve the impossible; but the last word on the subject surely comes from the nineteenth century through the mouth of Michael Davitt when giving evidence to the Gladstone Committee. As an Irish political offender he had had personal experience of penal servitude. " Of course man is a talking animal and no matter what rules you adopt to prevent talking, if you have a thousand men congregated in a prison they will insist on exercising this natural right to speak." [30]

Yet, for all their inhumanity and futility, the separate system and the silence rule did have one highly desirable object, the prevention of mutual contamination among the prisoners. Whatever view may be taken about the reformative potentialities of imprisonment, no one would be disposed

---

[28] Brocklehurst, *op. cit.* p. 103.
[29] *People in Prison*, para. 244.   [30] Minutes 11, pp. 268–269.

to doubt the existence of deformative risks, although it is equally true that no one knows much about their extent. They can be mitigated by segregation such as that of prisoners above and below the age of twenty-one which is still rigorously practised, and that between prisoners serving their first sentence and those more deeply steeped in prison life, which is perhaps less rigorously practised than used to be the case. But it is open to question whether the risk of contamination can be considerably reduced by anything short of a return to a rigorous form of the separate system which, save for very short periods, would be unacceptable on humanitarian grounds, even if it were practicable.

One way of counteracting the possible deformative effects of association with his brothers in misfortune is to provide the prisoner with other interests and the opportunity of communicating with other people. The first can be attempted by education in the broad sense, vocational training and work; the second by the provision of facilities for keeping in touch with the world outside prison and the regular communication on something more than disciplinary level with the prison staff.

No doubt there has been progress with regard to education and vocational training since 1895. So far as work is concerned, the achievements of convict labour in the nineteenth century must never be forgotten. They include the erection of Wormwood Scrubs between 1874 and 1890. The much vaunted building of the detention centre at Eastwood Park in Gloucestershire by prisoners brought to the site from Bristol and Leigh Hill prisons is no more than a pale replica. Nevertheless, the overall position is better today than it ever was in the nineteenth century, if only because of the total absence of productive labour in local prisons of those days.

But the most drastic changes are undoubtedly those which have taken place in the prisoners' contacts with the outside world and with the staff.

Gone are the days when the prisoner was dependent on his visitor for items of news, including the football results. In any prison in which he spends his leisure in association with other inmates, he now has access to radio, television and newspapers, and, in a cellular training prison, he may have a radio in his cell.[31] More important than these amenities is the possibility of home leave. At present it is only open to prisoners serving sentences of two years or more in training prisons, and then only towards the end of the sentence; but it is not unreasonable to anticipate further developments in this direction. Reference has already been made to the pre-release hostel system; this is only available to long term prisoners, but all prisoners may benefit from a visit from the welfare officer who will keep them in touch with their families through the local probation service, and who will be available for consultation on visits by the family to the prison. In some prisons these visits are allowed every fortnight, and, if ever the overcrowding problem is solved, it is likely that the permitted number of such visits will increase.

Changes in the present regime such as those which have just been mentioned have led Professor Norval Morris to predict with confidence that, before the end of the century, prison as we now know it will have become extinct, " though the word may live on to cover quite different social organisa-

[31] *People in Prison*, para. 37.

tions." [32]   Many may think that this goes too far, especially
when allowance is made for the long-term prisoners who are
at present placed in category A as the higest security risk—
prisoners whose escape would be highly dangerous to the
public or the police or to the security of the state; but the
prison department already takes the view that those who
have had the custody of prisoners have increasingly realised
the need to see the period inside as an interval between two
periods outside, and not the other way round.[33]   For most
offenders, prison is ceasing to be the near banishment that
a term of penal servitude was in the second half of the
nineteenth century.

More significant than any of the developments which
have been mentioned so far is the change in the official
picture of the staff–inmate relationship.   In 1895, unnecessary conversation between staff and prisoners was prohibited;
I have even heard it said that conversation between members
of the staff while on duty was also forbidden.   Relaxation
was slow; during the last few years, however, members of
the uniformed staff have been encouraged to get to know
their charges and to become involved in their problems.   In
many instances this no doubt improves relationships and
lessens the tension which can creep all too easily into prison
life; but something more than a willingness to help is required
if the staff is to break down the passive resistance of the
prison sub-culture.   Individual prisoners may wish to estab-
lish a helpful relationship with a particular officer, and they
may often succeed; but such things are taboo according to
the norms of the community of prisoners.   To quote a member
of the prison medical service:

---

[32] *Criminology in Transition* (ed. Tadeus Grogier, Howard Jones and
J. C. Spencer), p. 268.   [33] *People in Prison*, para. 90.

" The most powerful influence on the prisoner is the inmate culture with its prison code. This code is a set of sanctions imposed by the prisoners upon themselves through various forms of group pressure. Its rules are derived from the basic characteristics of prisoners, who as a group are inadequate, aggressive and preoccupied with immediate needs. The code is socially unacceptable; in fact, it is quite hostile to ordinary social standards. Not only is crime (apart from a few sexual offences) regarded as admirable, but the more professional the crime, the more honour is paid to the criminal. Good relations with individual officers are suspect unless the intention is to use this relationship to mislead the authorities." [34]

The latest answer to this challenge is group counselling. A small group of prisoners, say ten, meet a member of the staff regularly (say once a week) for an hour or an hour and a half. Members are free to discuss anything they like. It could be sport or the weather, but more often than not it is the members' problems.[35] The organisation of the prison may come under discussion; nothing is done to restrict criticism, but there is usually a rule that a member of staff must not be specifically mentioned. Group counselling is not a channel for remedying grievances, and the staff member of the group, usually spoken of as the " group counsellor " must reserve his discretion to make such use as he thinks fit of information revealed at a meeting. The staff holds separate meetings to consider the progress of counselling. It seems that tensions

---

[34] Group Work in Prisons and Borstals (H.M.S.O, 1966), p. 32,
[35] *Ibid*. p. 4.

are relieved and communications throughout the prison improved.[36]

A further answer to the problem of the sub-culture is provided by what is sometimes called the " Norwich system " because it had its rather modest origin in Norwich prison.[37] A group of prisoners becomes the special responsibility of a particular officer; he collects information and makes the assessment necessary for classification and parole; he gets to know the members of the group well and participates in their activities. Leading from this type of group, it is sometimes suggested that the prison of the future will consist of a number of small semi-independent groups, each living in separate buildings, and even working in separate shops.[38] The question is thus raised of the extent to which it will be either feasible or desirable for our prisons to be transformed into therapeutic communities.

Grendon Underwood.   The only prison which at present has claims to be so described is Grendon Underwood in Buckinghamshire.   Opened in 1962 it has, as I have said, already been described as " the brightest jewel in the penal system." [39]   It is a psychiatric prison, not a mental hospital; the inmates suffer from personality disorders as opposed to mental illnesses requiring treatment under the Mental Health Act.   Prisoners may be transferred to Grendon from any other prison, but their consent to the transfer is essential. If found unsuited to the regime they will be removed from Grendon.

---

[36] De Berka, " Group Counselling in Penal Institutions," Vol. 8, *British Journal of Criminology*, p. 22.
[37] Prison Commissioners Report 1956, App. 4.
[38] Klare, *Anatomy of Prison*, Chap. 21.
[39] p. 39, *supra.*

In 1969, when Tony Parker was preparing his excellent book, *The Frying Pan,* in which Grendon and its inmates are described in their own words, there were 150 prisoners and about the same number of staff. About two-thirds of the latter were uniformed officers, and the rest consisted of civilians ranging from psychiatrists to shorthand typists. About 70 per cent. of the inmates displayed psychopathic traits. Lest the 1 : 1 ratio of prisoner and staff should cause surprise, it must be added that Grendon is intended to be an experimental prison, the object being to gather information about certain types of disorder and the methods of treating them.

Grendon is a maximum security prison, but the regime is permissive. The prisoners are locked in their rooms (which they call cells) at night, but there is association throughout the day. There is no overcrowding. The prisoners do supervised work and take compulsory exercise as in other prisons, but the prisoner-staff relationship is much closer. Very great emphasis is placed on the groups which meet every day, and the entire community meets as a group once a week. A psychiatrist, together with members of the staff, is present at the group meetings, and, although they are encouraged to put their problems to their groups, prisoners have opportunities for individual interviews with psychiatrists.

It is too early to pronounce on the success of Grendon as an experimental psychiatric prison, but the question naturally arises whether it would not be possible to treat it as a model for future prisons. To quote from Mr. Parker's introduction to his book:

" If we are never going to be able to think of any more
satisfactory way of dealing with habitual prisoners [40]

---

[40] Most of the inmates of Grendon have records.

than by habitually imprisoning them, then it seems likely that in any foreseeable future prisons will all eventually become like this one, small maximum security units, in remote and inaccessible parts of the country from which the inmates cannot and do not escape and which can therefore allow a humane and permissive regime within." [41]

I venture to doubt the feasibility, desirability or likelihood of such a development. It would obviously be impossible to generalise the Grendon staff-prisoner ratio or anything like it, and, if most or even a substantial number of prisons were to be on the Grendon model, some limit would have to be placed on the right to reject the unwanted trouble maker; but, quite apart from these self-evident points, I must confess to a good deal of scepticism about converting prisons into therapeutic communities. The model is of course the mental hospital, but we are asked to imagine such a hospital in which people are detained against their will although they fall right outside the Mental Health Act, in which the detention may have to continue long after a cure has been effected, and in which the vast majority of the patients are not, and never have been, either mentally ill or subject to any form of namable or treatable personality disorder. Small prisons in which the group has a role to play may have a future, but I believe this will only be as places to which selected offenders can be sent. I beg leave to question the potency of the group as the answer to all our prison problems. (Needless to say these remarks are not intended to cast any doubt on the value of the work at Grendon Underwood.) As to the likelihood of our having more prisons on the Grendon model

[41] p. xv.

in a reasonably foreseeable future, all that need be said is that the government's building programme outlined in *People in Prison*, published in 1969, does not suggest that it is very great.

After-care. Even the briefest comparison of contemporary prison conditions with those which prevailed at the end of the nineteenth century would be incomplete without a mention of after-care. At the time of the Gladstone Report, the position of the offender on release would have varied according to whether he was a convict emerging from a public works prison, where he had spent the major portion of a sentence of penal servitude, or a prisoner coming out of a local prison after what, in all probability, would have been a very short sentence.

The convict's release would have been on licence, but the condition of that licence would have been periodical reporting to the police, not obedience to the helpful directions of a probation officer as in the case of the modern licence. He would probably have been paid a gratuity representing the amount earned for industry and good conduct under the marks system by which promotion from one stage to another was dependent on the achievement of so many marks.[42] The gratuity could not exceed £7 and would probably have been less. The released convict might have enlisted the aid of a charitable society, such as the Royal Society for the Assistance of Discharged Prisoners, but he would have had no contact with agents of the society while in prison.

Paragraphs 34 to 36 of the Gladstone Report revealed a state of utter chaos so far as the arrangements for aid on discharge from local prisons was concerned. Most prisons

[42] p. 14, *supra*.

had their own discharged prisoners' aid society, but there was a plethora of other societies. Some prisoners appeared to have enlisted the aid of more than one of them, there was no provision for pre-release interviews with agents of the societies, and there appears to have been a confusion of offers of assistance from a variety of quarters at the prison gates.

After an interesting history of partnership between the State and voluntary agencies, after-care is now the concern of the Probation and After-Care Service. Its officers are welfare officers in the prisons and they make contact with the prisoner well before his release. Any prisoner can volunteer for after-care. In the case of certain offenders after-care is compulsory. These are offenders who are under twenty-one at the time of their sentence, offenders released on parole, offenders serving an extended prison sentence, and offenders serving a sentence of life imprisonment. In these cases the release is on licence. The licence requires the offender to report to and be guided by a probation officer; the offender is subject to recall for the rest of his sentence if he breaks one of the conditions of the licence.

The discharged prisoner still enjoys the possibility of assistance from other sources. He may be befriended by a member of the prison staff (something which would have been unheard of at the time of the Gladstone Report), and the help of the probation officer may be supplemented by volunteers who will assist over such mundane matters as baby sitting, the collection of luggage, or the completion of forms. For discharged prisoners who have nowhere to go on release, there is the possibility of a state-aided voluntary after-care hostel.[43]

[43] *People in Prison*, paras. 108–113.

Although the post-release prospects of a prisoner are probably a good deal better than they were at the time of the Gladstone Report, I am most anxious not to suggest that all is well. So far as I am aware, there is no reason to suppose that the attitude of the public towards the ex-prisoner is any more kind now than it was in 1895. After all, it was presumably in the 1950s that Hugh Klare, until very recently the secretary of the Howard League for Penal Reform, was asked whether he fumigated his bed linen after he had had ex-prisoners to stay with him.[44] How many of us can say that we have never adopted the " we and they " approach to questions concerning the ex-prisoner? How many employers can cross their hearts and swear that, when confronted with the choice between an ex-prisoner and another person a little less suitable for the post, they have not ignored the little difference? Is it beyond the bounds of reason that we should have legislation, on the analogy of the Disabled Persons Employment Act, under which certain firms are obliged to employ a quota of ex-prisoners?

The extent to which prison conditions are reformatory. I think that all the improvements in prison conditions mentioned in this lecture can properly be said to have been measures of penal reform. It will be recollected that I described a change in the penal system as " penal reform " if its aim can be brought under either of the two heads of (i) the rehabilitation or (ii) the more humane treatment of the offender. The abolition of degrading labour, the improvement in food, the increase in the association of prisoners, and the strengthening of their contacts with the outside world, all come under the second head, and their aim has

[44] Klare, *Anatomy of Prison*, p. 12.

been achieved. Imprisonment is a more humane institution than it was at the time of the Gladstone Report. Improvements with regard to work, education and vocational training can at least be said to have had a rehabilitative intent, although it is easy to exaggerate the extent to which this aim can be achieved by these means. It is common knowledge that a prisoner who works well inside is often not prepared to work at all outside. Education in prison may amount to little more than filling in time, and comparatively few prisoners are fit for vocational training although work, such as building done in prison, can lead to work of the same kind on discharge.[45] The change in the relationship between prisoners and staff can be regarded as humanitarian with a rehabilitative tinge, while, at any rate for some participants, group counselling may promote rehabilitation as well as the relaxation of tensions.

I am thus in a position to report progress to the shade of Emma Hamlyn. The twentieth century has witnessed the development of a more generous penal theory by Ewing at the expense of Stephen, the abolition of corporal and capital punishment, and the growth of prison conditions which, however deplorable they remain, are considerably less degrading than they were at the time of the Gladstone Report and for a long while after its publication. If anyone is inclined to doubt this, let him re-read Paterson's account of Dartmoor quoted at p. 30. Nevertheless, I must confess to profound scepticism about the extent to which prison can truly be said to be reformatory. This is due to my invincible armchair doubts about the extent to which it is possible to influence the future behaviour of mentally normal adults by acceptable artificially contrived means *while they are in*

---

[45] *People in Prison*, para. 61.

prison. Sir Alexander Paterson seems to me to have been right. It *is* impossible to train men for freedom in a condition of captivity.[46] In some cases reform may be brought about by a change of heart which may be either sudden or the outcome of reflection; in other cases the erstwhile offender simply drifts out of crime through the acquisition of other interests or mere maturation. The change of heart, acquisition of other interests, or maturation, can, and no doubt sometimes does, occur in prison; but they are much more likely to occur outside owing, for example, to the influence of a friend, the guidance of a probation officer, membership of a sympathetic group, matrimony or change of employment. The chances of deterioration in prison are at least as great as those of reform; surely the most realistic approach is to regard the rehabilitative changes mentioned in this lecture as aimed primarily at the prevention of deterioration. If analogies have to be drawn, prisons are more like cold storage depots than either therapeutic communities or training institutions. To quote from Alexander Paterson yet again: " A man is not primarily sent to prison in order that he may be reformed." In my next lecture I will suggest that the belief that people can be reformed by being sent to prison has had a baneful influence on the length of prison sentences.

My rather damping conclusion that the main aim of prison reform should be the prevention of prisoners' deterioration must not be taken to reflect in any way on the work of the prison department. The prevention of deterioration is just as important as the promotion of reform, and the methods of achieving the two objects are similar. From the theoretical point of view the correct analysis seems to be that people are sent to prison as a symbol of the community's disapproval

[46] p. 33, *supra.*

of their conduct in order that they and others may be deterred from crime, and for the protection of the public from their depredations while they are in prison. There is also the admittedly remote possibility that the catharsis of punishment will effect a reformation; then there is the hope that reform will be brought about by prison discipline, but this is incidental to, not the object of, the imprisonment. The imprisonment is for the benefit of the public, and the public is under a duty to do all that reasonably can be done to prevent the permanent moral degradation of the prisoner. There is a real danger that someone who is already a bad man when he goes into prison will come out worse; hence the crucial importance of what can best be described as " anti-deformative action " in our prisons.

Hence too the desirability of insuring that the period of imprisonment should be as short as it possibly can be compatibly with the aims of the sentence whether they be denunciation, deterrence, the protection of the public or all three. This is a matter to which I turn at the beginning of my next lecture.

THE REDUCTION AND AVOIDANCE OF IMPRISONMENT AND PUNISHMENT

1. THE REDUCTION OF IMPRISONMENT

Remission. It is common knowledge that English prison sentences do not mean what they say. The judge announces to the convicted criminal that the sentence will be three years imprisonment; the criminal, like everyone else in court, probably knows perfectly well that he will only spend two years "inside," provided he behaves himself. The period of remission for industry and good conduct derives from the ticket of leave of the days of transportation [1]; its duration has varied from time to time and according to the type of sentence. The effect of rule 5 of the Prison Rules 1964 is that it is now a third of every sentence of imprisonment of more than forty-five days.[2] Release on remission of a prisoner serving a fixed term sentence is generally not on licence. The result is that, however long his sentence may have been, he is not subject to any supervision unless he volunteers for after-care. And he cannot, in any circumstances, be recalled to serve the last third of his sentence. Under section 61 of the Criminal Justice Act 1967, the Home Secretary may, subject to very important restrictions mentioned later, release a person serving a sentence of life imprisonment at any time, but the release is on licence and the licence will last for the rest of the prisoner's life.

---

[1] p. 8, *supra.*
[2] There is no remission of a sentence of 31 days or less, and remission may not reduce the period of incarceration below 31 days.

Even in the case of fixed-term sentences, there are two exceptional classes of prisoner whose release on remission must be on licence, *viz.* the offender who was under twenty-one at the commencement of his sentence, and the persistent offender subject to an extended sentence of imprisonment.[3] But it is arguable that someone who has been in prison for a continuous period of, say, four years (the length of sentence mentioned in the abortive section 20 of the Criminal Justice Act 1961) should, when released on remission, be put on terms under which he will be subject to supervision and to liability to recall for the residue of his sentence for breach of a condition of the licence.   There are arguments both ways.   In favour of the suggestion it can be urged that there is some evidence that prisoners with a tendency to recidivism do better when released on licence than would otherwise be the case,[4] and it is not difficult to imagine circumstances in which the possibility of recall would be greatly in the public interest; obvious instances are the violent offender known to be besetting the house of his amatory rival, the robber known to be associating with his former gang, and the sex offender convicted of some trifling indecency which is not, of itself, thought to merit imprisonment.   Against the suggestion it can be urged that it is undesirable to augment a class of the community which is, in effect, liable to imprisonment for conduct which either does not constitute an offence or else is not of itself thought to be sufficiently grave to merit imprisonment.   The following figures relating to state prisons in California are said to cause concern in some quarters in that state.   Of the 7,685 felons committed to State prisons in 1969, 2,661 were recalls from parole; and of these 1,946 were

---

[3] Criminal Justice Act 1967, s. 60 (3).
[4] Hammond and Chayen, *Persistent Criminals* (1963, H.M.S.O.).

recalled without fresh commitment for another offence.[5] The administration of our own parole system to date does not point to the likelihood of such figures in this country, but the danger is one to be kept in mind. Further points that can be urged against the suggestion are that the needs of long term prisoners are now adequately catered for by hostel schemes, and that the proposal would add to the already excessive burden of the Probation and After-care Service. But it is not every long term prisoner who finishes his sentence in a hostel and, in any event, living in a prison hostel is not the same thing as living in the community. As to the burden on the Probation and After-care Service, I will shortly be urging that it is imperative that something should be done towards replenishing the numbers as well as the pockets of this under-manned and under-paid body. We have reached a position in which there cannot be all that much change in the treatment of offenders without increasing the work of the probation service. On the whole I think that the arguments in favour of the suggestion that the release on remission of long fixed-term prisoners should be on licence outweigh the arguments to the contrary; but a possible compromise would be to do everything possible to encourage these prisoners to volunteer for after-care. This would give them the benefit of supervision without the draconian threat of recall. In any event, there is evidence that the number of volunteers for after-care is increasing.[6]

The main purpose of remission for industry and good conduct is of course the maintenance of discipline in prison, and, whatever changes are made in the prison regime in the future, it seems likely that something of the kind will persist.

[5] *Crime and Delinquency in California* 1969.
[6] *People in Prison*, para. 107.

It only introduces a very small element of indeterminacy into a prison sentence for, in the case of a fixed-term sentence, it is possible to inform the prisoner on reception of the exact date on which he will be released if he behaves himself even if he is not granted parole.

Parole.   " Parole is the discharge of prisoners from custody in advance of their expected date of release, provided they agree to abide by certain conditions, so that they may serve some portion of their sentences under supervision in the community, but subject to recall for misconduct." [7]   Any-one serving a fixed term sentence of eighteen months or more is entitled to be considered for release on licence which could run from the date when he has served a third of his sentence or a year, whichever is the longer. The licence will normally last until the date when the prisoner would have been entitled to release without licence on remission, *i.e.*, at the expiration of two-thirds of his sentence; but in the case of prisoners who were under twenty-one when their sentences began and those serving an extended sentence, it may endure throughout the entirety of the sentence. During the currency of his licence the parolee is subject to recall for breach of any of its conditions. The conditions may be of a general kind, requiring the offender to report regularly to the probation officer, to lead an honest and industrious life, etc. or they may be more specific, such as a requirement to reside in a particular place, to undergo medical treatment, or to complete a course of vocational training begun in prison. Someone serving life sentence may be released on licence at any time. A prisoner serving a fixed term sentence to whom parole

---

[7] Report of the Parole Board for 1968, para. 5.

was refused on the first consideration of his case is entitled to what is, in effect, an annual review in consequence of which he has a further chance of parole.

It will be seen that parole differs from remission in three respects. It always entails a licence, it is granted, if at all, at an earlier date and, most important of all, it is not something to which the prisoner is entitled as of right. He must apply for it and, judging from the 1970 figures, the chances are about seven to three against his getting it on first application. Parole also differs from remission in its history and (perhaps) in the fact that it is not reflected in the sentences of the courts.

Remission, as we have seen, goes far back into the nineteenth century. The release on licence from penal servitude which could, in theory, be earned by all convicts at the same stage of their sentence, although there must have been much variation in practice, derives from the transportee's ticket of leave. The remission without licence of imprisonment derives, in its turn, from the release on licence of penal servitude. The discretionary release on licence known as parole is, on the other hand, very modern so far as Great Britain is concerned. The account I am giving of the subject is based on sections 59 to 62 of the Criminal Justice Act 1967 and rules made thereunder. It is our first parole statute but, if we have been a little behind the times in this respect, I think the scheme we have adopted has the makings of a very good one. My ideal parole system would add a little more to the indeterminacy of a fixed-term sentence by authorising release on licence at any time during the first two-thirds of the term; but we may come to that. It has already been suggested that what is called the " threshold " period should be reduced to eight months. It is by no means impossible that the requirement that a third of the sentence should be spent in prison will disappear in time, although this would involve a considerable increase in the size and number of functions of the Parole Board.   I attach great importance to the preservation, under our system, of the courts' power to fix the maximum of a man's sentence.   Life sentences have a useful part to play, and it may be that there should be more of them, but I would like them to continue to be most exceptional.[8]   I applaud the preservation of the courts' power since, to hand all prisoners over to the Executive as final arbiter of the duration of their sentence would be to rob the courts of their traditional role as the protector of the liberties of the subject.   To my mind this objection is equally valid if the Executive is made to appoint sentencing boards under some such scheme as that canvassed by last year's Hamlyn lecturer.[9]   To give the Executive power to modify a sentence, especially a long sentence, is another matter; it promotes the liberty of the subject instead of curtailing it.   For this reason I am glad that our system does not, as the parole laws of some parts of the United States and British Commonwealth do, empower the courts to fix a minimum which must be served in prison together with a maximum which may be served (with or without remission).   Under such a system the judge says to the prisoner, " Your sentence is X years, you will become eligible for parole after X minus Y years." There is always the risk that Y will be too small a quantity.

It is too early to say whether the possibility of release on parole has led to an overall increase in the length of prison sentences.   In paragraph 108 of the second report of the

---

[8] 130 life sentences were imposed in 1970, and that seems to have been an all-time high.

[9] *The English Judge* by Henry Cecil, p. 132.

Parole Board which covers the year 1969 it is said that there is no evidence that the scheme has been at all influential in changing the courts' approach to sentencing. In answer to a question, put by an inmate of Hull prison, as to why every prisoner should not be given the chance of at least a certain period on parole, the report says:

> " The questioner had not apparently considered that such a policy would do away with the difference between parole and automatic remission of sentence; and that automatic remission would be duly reflected, as parole is emphatically not, in the sentences meted out by the courts."

The implication that automatic remission is reflected in the length of sentence is interesting because there is authority for the proposition that it should not be taken into account by the courts.[10] On the other hand, the increase in remission to its present quantity of a third, which took place during the Second World War, may have reacted on the judicial subconscious in such a way as to be partly responsible for the increase in the annual average length of sentence, which took place between 1938 and 1948, to which I shall shortly be referring.

The decision to grant or withhold parole is sometimes spoken of as " a hole and corner conclusion reached un-judicially by civil servants behind closed doors." But this is a travesty of the truth. Each prison has attached to it a local review committee, the members of which include, in addition to the governor and a representative of the prison's Board of Visitors who will most probably be a magistrate, a probation officer together with some other person who is in

---

[10] *R.* v. *Maguire* (1956) 40 Cr.App.R. 92.

no way connected with the prison. These committees consider the cases of all inmates serving fixed-term sentences who will shortly become eligible for parole, and of all those who, having been refused parole in the past, are entitled to a further review. The local review committees' recommendations are passed on to the Parole Board which also considers some of the local rejects. The membership of the Parole Board under the chairmanship of Lord Hunt, is broadly based; it includes high court judges, psychiatrists, social workers, criminologists, a retired member of the prison department and a retired police officer.

It is true that the decision to release is the Home Secretary's, but he can only release on the recommendation of the Parole Board, although he may decide against release notwithstanding such a recommendation; this latter course is seldom adopted.[11] It is also true that the decision to refer the case of a lifer to the Parole Board is made in the Home Office, but the Home Secretary can only release on the recommendation of the Board and after consulting the Lord Chief Justice together with a trial judge if available. It is also true that the prisoner is not represented when his case is considered by either the review committee or the Parole Board, but these bodies have to consider any written representations the prisoner may wish to make, and he must be interviewed by a member of the local review committee. Finally it is true that the Board does not tell the prisoner its reasons for refusing parole. Prisoners urge that this should be done, otherwise they cannot know what is expected of them. To this the answer is that the reasons for parole decisions are by no means exclusively dependent on what the prisoner can

[11] It was only adopted in two cases in 1970.

do. The sad truth is that someone who has numerous previous convictions, a bad work record, and an all too short trouble-free period following his last release from custody, is a poor parole risk. There is little he can do while in prison to show that, though he belongs to a class of which the majority will recidivate, he is in the minority. Even in the case of such a person, parole may be granted close to the end of the second third of his sentence in order to secure for him the benefit of supervision and the stimulus of liability to recall during the early days of freedom. In fact, there are those who say, seemingly most unjustly, that the Parole Board achieves an inflated success rate by concentrating on those who do not have much time to serve before they will be entitled to release on remission without licence.

The annual reports of the Board very definitely give the lie to the picture of parole provided by Ruggles-Brise.[12] Reliance is not placed " merely on the observation of a prisoner while in prison." Dossiers have to be considered, and account is taken of the matters mentioned in the last paragraph together with many others, such as the nature of the offence, the public alarm caused by it, the observations of the trial judge, the prisoner's prospects on release and his domestic circumstances. All this involves the perusal of reports, discussions and interviews to such an extent that it has become necessary to arrange for meetings of the Parole Board to take place in Manchester and Birmingham as well as London. Still more decentralisation may become necessary; it may even be found desirable to let the local review committees make the final recommendation in the case of relatively short sentences of, say, two or even three years.

[12] p. 24, *supra.*

At the beginning of their first report the members of the Parole Board expressed the view that the introduction of parole would come to be regarded as "a milestone on the main road of progress." I cordially agree with this assessment. Naturally the Board is proceeding with extreme caution, but the periodic reviews which the system entails may provide the answer to some criticisms of our sentencing system and to some suggestions that are made with regard to it. For example, it is frequently said that a judge is not the best person to fix the length of a prison sentence because he is ignorant of the likely effect of imprisonment upon the offender. The remedy, it is said, is to have sentencing (or treatment) boards composed of those who are likely to be better informed in this regard. I have already referred to my objection to this proposal on the ground that it would rob the courts of their traditional role of protectors of the liberty of the subject; to deprive the English judge of his sentencing duties would be to change the nature of his office because judges have been the sole sentencers of English criminals throughout the ages. Such a drastic change would only be justified by the most cogent evidence of a preferable alternative and this brings me to my second objection to the proposal. In the case, at any rate, of mentally normal adult offenders, there is no evidence that anyone else is any less ignorant than the judge of the likely effect of imprisonment on the particular offender. In the present state of knowledge, it must, *faute de mieux*, be a case of wait and see; but this is no argument against periodical reviews of the case and herein, to my mind, lies the real importance of the introduction of parole.

It has tended to reduce the prison population in the sense that, after the release of the first parolee, there would have been more people in prison had parole not been introduced; but it would be quite wrong to regard prison emptying as the object of this part of the Criminal Justice Act 1967, or as a dominant consideration in the minds of the members of the Parole Board when deciding whether to grant or withhold release on licence in a particular case. In paragraph 49 of its first report the Board acknowledged the assistance derived from the following statement in paragraph 5 of the White Paper entitled *The Adult Offender* published in 1965 [13] in which the introduction of parole was proposed:

> " A considerable number of long-term prisoners reach a recognisable peak in their training at which they may respond to generous treatment, but after which, if kept in prison, they may go downhill. To give such prisoners the opportunity of supervised freedom at the right moment may be decisive in securing their return to decent citizenship."

This suggests that the object of parole is the reduction of recidivism by giving generous treatment to carefully selected prisoners. It would be premature to attempt to assess the extent to which the object is being achieved, although the third report of the Parole Board does suggest that those who have been released on licence are doing a little better after their licence has expired than they would have been expected to do had they been released on remission without licence.

There is scepticism in some quarters about the recognisable peak, but it is possible to state the case for parole in terms of the reduction of punishment. The prevention of

---

[13] Cmd. 2852. In para. 9, parole is commended as an incentive to reform and as something which would militate against overcrowding in prisons.

recidivism is not the sole object of imprisonment. Regard must be had to such other considerations as the protection of the public by the removal of a dangerous offender from circulation, the deterrence of others and the importance of emphasising the gravity of the offence. If, compatibly with these considerations, it proves possible to release a number of prisoners at an earlier date than that at which they were entitled to expect to be released on quitting the dock, parole will have justified itself even though the reconviction rate of the parolees is no lower than that which would have been expected had they been released on remission. It will be recollected that the reduction of punishment was among the criteria of penal reform mentioned at the beginning of my second lecture.

Length of sentences. This leads on to the thorny topic of the length of prison sentences, a sphere in which I believe there has been some regress rather than progress in penal reform during the twentieth century. There are two humanitarian reasons for ensuring that sentences are as short as they can be compatibly with the needs of deterring the offender and making allowance for the other objects of imprisonment which I have mentioned (the protection of the public, general deterrence, and a denunciation of the offence). The first is the obvious one of minimising the suffering of the offender and his family; the second, which is only slightly less obvious, is the desirability of improving the lot of other prisoners by reducing overcrowding. The daily average population of the prisons is affected by the length of sentences meted out as well as by the number of people sentenced.

It is the vast increase in the average length of sentence

which took place between 1938 and 1958 which leads me to believe that there has been some regress rather than progress in penal reform during this century. I say "some" advisedly because I realise that most of this increase is attributable to the spectacular reduction of the number of extremely short sentences of a fortnight or less imposed mainly on fine defaulters and drunks; but notably in the period 1938–48 there were significant increases in the number of sentences from three to six, six to twelve and twelve to eighteen months. Two causes suggest themselves. The first is the increase in remission which took place towards the beginning of the 1939 war, and I say no more about this. Even if remission is something which the judge ought not to take into account when fixing a particular sentence, it is difficult to believe that an increase in its amount would have no effect on his sentencing over a period.

The second cause of the increase in sentences of three months and more that occurs to me is the confidence, so vociferously expressed at the time, in the reformative potential of comparatively prolonged imprisonment. The period was one of penological optimism, and the stage was set by Dr. Mannheim's advocacy in 1939 of a ban on institutional treatment of less than three months duration,[14] together with the assertion, which for aught I know still holds good, by Hubert and East, that a sentence of less than six months is insufficient for psychiatric treatment.[15] Confidence in the merits of comparatively prolonged imprisonment persisted. Winifred Elkin was doing no more than expressing the penological spirit of the age in the following comment on the fact

[14] *The Dilemma of Penal Reform*, p. 225.
[15] *The Psychological Treatment of Crime* (H.M.S.O. 1939), para. 171.

that, in 1953, more than two-thirds of the men and 84 per cent. of the women sent to prison got sentences of less than six months:

> " It is quite impossible that the prisons should be able to exert any effective reformative influence in so short a time, nor is the fear of a short sentence likely to have any deterrent effect. It is a startling, but incontrovertible, fact that for the majority of prisoners, imprisonment serves no useful purpose, either from the angle of deterrence or reformation. It is only an indication that society disapproves of a certain type of behaviour." [16]

These words were written in 1957. The comment would have been equally appropriate if it had been made in 1967 for, in that year, over 70 per cent. of the total number of prison sentences imposed were for periods of six months or less.[17] The length of sentences for the following years has been affected by the introduction of suspended sentences, the reduction of imprisonment for default in payment of fines and the increased powers of fining for each of which provision was made in the Criminal Justice Act 1967. Even so, over 59 per cent. of the sentences passed in 1968, and more than 50 per cent. of those passed in 1969, were for six months or less. But Miss Elkin's comment must now be regarded as inappropriate because we have moved into an era of penological pessimism. We are now told that the results of research to date indicate that longer institutional sentences are no more effective in preventing recidivism than

---

[16] *The English Penal System*, p. 124 (1957).
[17] *People in Prison*, table 5. The figure includes fine defaulters but without them it would still have been 61 per cent. (See Prison Department Report for 1970.)

shorter ones.[18]   I must also take leave to question Miss
Elkin's assertion that short sentences are ineffective as an
individual deterrent.   It is a well known fact that a very
high proportion of those who serve a prison sentence for the
first time do not return to prison.   The 1957 edition of
Prisons and Borstals, current at the time of the publication
of Miss Elkin's book, said that the proportion was as much
as three quarters.   It is reasonable to suppose that many of
these first timers received sentences of six months or less.
Surely it is also reasonable to suppose that they were
deterred by the experience of imprisonment.

Let me now enlarge on my point with regard to the baneful influence of the myth that prison is reformative by a brief
reference to some of the information to be gathered from
tables 1 to 5 of *People in Prison,* published by the Home
Office in 1969.   Taking the 1961 figure as an index of 100,
the average length of sentence for 1938 was 38·9, that for
1948 82·7, and that for 1958 98·8.   The following figures are
striking confirmation of the fact that the increase was
primarily due to the decrease in very short sentences.   Of
the 30,646 receptions under sentence (including fine defaulters) in 1938 8,820 (28·7 per cent.) were for periods of two
weeks or less.   The corresponding figures for 1948 were
35,277 receptions, 3,366 (10 per cent.) for two weeks or less.
24·4 per cent. of the 1938 sentences were for periods of over
two and up to five weeks; by 1948, the percentage had been
reduced to 16·7 per cent.   But the following account for
part of the increase in the average length of sentence between
1938 and 1948: increases of from 12·9 per cent. to 18·3 per
cent. and 6·1 per cent. to 14·3 per cent. respectively in the

---

[18] Hood and Sparks, *Key Issues in Criminology,* p. 190.

number of sentences of over three and up to six months, and over six and up to twelve months.   The 1948 percentages of sentences from over twelve to eighteen months and from over eighteen months to three years rose in each case from approximately 2 per cent. to 7 per cent.   The 1958 figures show an increase of about 1 per cent. in the number of sentences of from over three and up to six months and from over eighteen months and up to three years.   The increase has been maintained.   Expressed in terms of a percentage of the 1961 figure, 1958 was a peak year until 1968, but the average length never sank as low as that of 1948.

Assuming that my point that part of the increase in the average length of sentence between 1938 and 1958 was due to the contemporary belief that prison could be reformative if only the authorities were given enough time is the valid one, what should be done about it?   A plausible answer would be, pass a statute embodying Professor Norval Morris' principle that the maximum of a man's punishment should never be greater than the amount which would be justified by other aims of our criminal justice than that of reform [19]; but this would not do because it is very doubtful whether a judge ever says to himself " On all other grounds my sentence would be four months, but it would be six months in this case because two extra months are necessary for the sake of reform."   What is needed is a change in judicial practice.   If there is anything in the point that the 1938–58 increase was due to the voice of the penological optimist, the only chance of procuring an overall shortening of sentences seems to be the preaching of penological pessimism —the constant reiteration of the proposition that all the

[19] p. 56, *supra.*

judge can hope to achieve by a prison sentence is deterrence of the offender and others, together with whatever degree of protection of the public is thought appropriate in the circumstances.[20]   At the level of sentencing which I have been so far considering (periods of three years and less) the protection of the public is necessarily limited, although every little counts.   As to deterrence, although common sense tells us that five years is a greater deterrent than one, it is a good deal less explicit on the question whether three years is more of a deterrent than two, eighteen months more than a year, or a year more than six months.   If it is granted that reformative potential is irrelevant to the length of a prison sentence, we should, I think, do well to err, if err we must, on the side of leniency.

Reference to common sense prompts me to plead for the acceptance of a general rule that the first prison sentence should be a short one (say, no more than three months).   Of course I realise that there may be offences, especially those tried by the higher courts, the gravity of which calls for a substantial sentence, but I base my plea for short first sentences on one of the few facts with regard to the efficacy of penal measures as to which there is a high degree of certainty.   I have already said that a very large proportion of those who go to prison for the first time, whether it be on their first conviction or only after other measures have been tried, are not sent there again for a long time, if at all.   The figure is variously stated.   It is probably not so high now as the 87 per cent. of male releases and 89 per cent. of female releases mentioned in the White Paper *Penal Practice in a Changing Society* published in 1959.[21]   It has been variously

[20] p. 158, *infra.*   [21] p. 38, *supra.*

stated before and since. We have seen that three-quarters was the figure mentioned in the 1957 edition of *Prisons and Borstals*; in paragraph 67 of the third report of the Parole Board it is said that 70 per cent. of those who serve a prison sentence for the first time do not offend again. Some statements do not make it plain whether the reference is to first offenders or to those undergoing imprisonment for the first time, but even if the proportion of non-returners is as low as 62 per cent.[22] common sense indicates that the first prison sentence should generally be a short one.

I believe in following the dictates of common sense in the absence of a compelling reason to the contrary, but, in this instance, some may think that there is just such a reason in the results of the research done by Dr. Hammond for the Scottish Advisory Council on the Treatment of Offenders whose report on the use of short sentences by the courts was published in 1960.[23] Of the 3,163 Scottish male first offenders over seventeen included in Dr. Hammond's sample, the number of reconvictions after a three-year follow-up was below the expected rate, having regard to the age and offence of the offender, in the case of those sentenced to imprisonment for six months or more, but higher in the case of those sentenced for lesser periods. I would, however, be very loth to deduce from this research a general rule that the first prison sentence should always be for six months or more. I would require a large quantity of very clear evidence in favour of its superior efficacy before canvassing a rule which would lead to what would be a drastic increase of the average length of the first prison sentence.

---

[22] This figure comes from the sample of men serving their first prison sentence studied in Charmian Blackler's article on primary recidivism in 8 *British Journal of Criminology* (1968), p. 158. [23] App. F.

Those who are given to enlarging on the severity of our criminal law are apt to convey the impression that the English judge spends his days passing long sentences, with the result that our prisons are teeming with inmates who have little hope of freedom for a considerable time to come. Nothing could be further from the truth. In 1968 only 364 offenders received fixed-term sentences of more than five years, and, of these sentences, only fifty-four were for ten years or more.[24] On December 31, 1970, only 237 prisoners were serving fixed sentences of more than ten years; on the same day 753 life sentences were being served. The number of people who received life sentences in 1970 was 130. Only ·043 per cent. of the 34,371 receptions under sentence in 1968 were in respect of sentences for ten years or more (including life).[25]

Life sentences differ from those for a fixed term in that they are subject to preliminary reviews by the Home Office in order to determine when the case should be referred to the local review committee with a view to an ultimate release on licence. Each case is carefully considered at a very early stage; a review is normally fixed for the fourth year of the sentence and it is generally at a further review during the seventh year that it is decided to refer the case to the local review committee. When it is recommended, release of a lifer on licence is usually fixed for a date about a year ahead to enable the prisoner to be prepared for freedom by transfer to a hostel or open prison. The practice does, however, vary considerably. In *People in Prison* we are told

[24] 72 in 1970.
[25] The 1970 figures are taken from Lord Windlesham's statement in the House of Lords on February 17, 1971 (H.L. Debates, Vol. 315, col. 625), the remaining figures in this paragraph come from *People in Prison* and the Prison Department's Report of 1970.

that, since the war, most life sentence prisoners have served a term equal to that served by a prisoner with a long fixed sentence of from ten to eighteen years on which the normal remission of one-third is granted, but it is recognised that the position is changing as a result of the abolition of capital punishment for murder, and I shall have more to say on this point in my last lecture.

At this stage I simply want to suggest that prisoners serving sentences of ten years or more should be treated as a special category from the point of view of parole. Let it be granted that they must be considered for parole, if they so desire, as the end of the first third of their sentence approaches; if they are refused parole at the first review, let the date of the next review be fixed either by the local review committee, or by the Parole Board, or by the Home Office. In this way the agony of repeated annual applications by the prisoner himself could be avoided. I think the suggestion would meet with the approval of the chairman of the Parole Board, Lord Hunt.[26]

Although there are not many of them, long prison sentences give rise to qualms on humanitarian grounds. This point was well put by Lord Donaldson in the House of Lords debate concerning long prison sentences. Having doubted whether fourteen years is a greater deterrent than ten, though recognising that six years is a greater deterrent than two, he said:

"But one can say that if you ever give more than ten years' sentence you are not increasing the deterrent in any way. I would also say that if you are doing something, which there is a good deal of evidence to show is

26 H.L. Debates, Vol. 315, col. 640.

cruel, and there is any way of avoiding it, then you should avoid it." [27]

Lord Donaldson proceeded to propose legislation to the effect that, if a judge were minded to pass a sentence in excess of ten years, he should do so in terms of a minimum and maximum, and the minimum should never exceed five years.

Of course we are all at sea when it comes to estimating the deterrent effects of the different fixed-term sentences, and empowering the judge to pass a minimum as well as a maximum sentence would be a departure from English practice, although there are many precedents from abroad. The point is that there is a growing body of opinion that, notwithstanding the introduction of parole, some limit, other than the statutory maximum which, in the case of serious offences, is often life, should be placed on the judge's power to fix the length of a prison sentence. Speaking in a somewhat conservative vein for myself, I would approve a provision according to which all sentences in excess of ten years should be wholly indeterminate, *i.e.* life sentences; but I would gladly settle for a lower figure and, if obliged to go above ten, I would suggest fourteen years as long as that period continues to be the only significant statutory maximum between ten years and life which can be imposed for any offence. This would mean that, even if parole were never granted, the maximum period of incarceration would be between nine and ten years; we must never forget that Sir Alexander Paterson gravely doubted whether an average man could serve more than ten continuous years' imprisonment without deterioration.[28] If this kind of proposal were to attract considerable opposition, an alternative would be to

[27] *Ibid.* col. 660.   [28] p. 57, *supra*.

give the judge the choice, in cases in which the present maximum is life, between a fixed-term sentence up to ten years or life with a recommended minimum as in the case of murder.

Having begun this section with talk of regress, I should finish it by drawing attention to progress in a humanitarian direction in relation to the type of offence which attracts a long sentence. Gone are the days when a farm labourer with one previous conviction for theft could be given seven years penal servitude for stealing twelve eggs from under a duck.[29] The number of people serving sentences of penal servitude was reduced from 4,029 in 1899 to 1,308 in 1921 with the result that Portland could be closed as a convict prison.

2. The Avoidance of Imprisonment

Writing in 1922, Sydney and Beatrice Webb said in their *English Prisons under Local Government*:

> " We suspect that it passes the wit of man to contrive a prison which shall not be gravely injurious to the minds of the vast majority of prisoners, if not also to their bodies. So far as can be seen at present, the most practical and hopeful of 'prison reforms' is to keep people out of prison altogether." [30]

I am sure there are those who would be disposed to question the first sentence, especially in the case of comparatively short term prisoners; but I doubt whether there are many who would wish to quarrel with the second. Even if imprison-

[29] Anon., *Five Years Penal Servitude*, p. 300. Between 1864 and 1891 sentences of penal servitude could not be less than five years for the first offence and seven years for the second but a short period of imprisonment was an alternative.

[30] p. 248.

ment has no permanent detrimental effect on a prisoner, it means loss of employment, temporary, if not permanent, loss of wife and family, the risk of contamination and impaired ability to get further employment. Small wonder then that prison has come to be regarded as the sentencer's last resort. The fine has been available as an alternative in less serious cases for a very long time though not, in the case of all felonies, until the Criminal Justice Act 1948 came into force. Probation and discharges were, as we have seen, mainly the product of this century; and the suspended sentence is a very recent innovation. These measures are available to the courts in the case of all offences punishable with imprisonment, but, in addition, there are restrictions on the imprisonment of those below the age of twenty-one [31] and first offenders,[32] while special provisions exist for mentally abnormal offenders.[33] Most of these are also the outcome of twentieth century legislation, and, as it is even more humane not to send an offender to prison at all, than to ensure that his period of incarceration is as brief as possible, it can undoubtedly be said that there has been progress in penal reform in this sphere in the twentieth century; but the fact remains that the provision of further alternatives to imprisonment is still the penal reformer's most insistent demand.

Probation and the probation officer. I do not wish to add to what I have already said about the history of pro-

---

[31] p. 21, *supra.*
[32] The First Offenders Act 1958 prohibits magistrates' courts from sentencing first offenders to imprisonment unless of opinion that no other method of dealing with them is appropriate.
[33] Mental Health Act 1959, s. 60 (hospital and guardianship orders) and s. 71 (detention at Her Majesty's pleasure on acquittal on the ground of insanity).

bation.[34]   It has come to be used fairly extensively by the courts in the case of all kinds of offenders.   Nine per cent. of the 27,549 sentences passed by Assizes and Quarter Sessions in 1969 on offenders over the age of twenty-one consisted of probation orders, as did 8 per cent. of the 137,283 sentences imposed by magistrates' courts on such offenders after summary trial of indictable offences.   The 1 per cent. may not seem to be much of a difference, but it leads one to wonder whether magistrates might not make more use of probation and less of imprisonment.   The only point about which I do want to add something concerns the present lot of the probation officer.

Speaking of the Probation of Offenders Act 1907 in his *Struggle for Penal Reform*, Dr. Gordon Rose says that even the Home Office did not see that, in passing the Act, they had created a new profession.[35]   The oversight has of course been made good for a considerable time, and no one has any doubts today about the important and honourable nature of the profession of probation officer.   What is overlooked is the variety of the probation officer's duties in relation to the penal system, and the enormous significance of the role which he will have to play if we really are going to make a serious attempt at the provision of further alternatives to imprisonment.

The supervision of convicted offenders committed immediately to their care is, though in itself enough to constitute a whole-time job, but one aspect of the work of the members of the probation and after-care service.   As the name of the service implies, a further aspect is the after-care of discharged prisoners who have either been released

[34] p. 19, *supra.*
[35] p. 82.

on licence or else volunteered for after-care.[36] It follows that the introduction of parole has added considerably to the work of the service. A further aspect of the work of its members is the preparation of social inquiry reports to assist the courts in pronouncing sentence, a task which is most certainly likely to increase rather than decrease. Then there is the welfare work to be done in relation to the prisoner while he is inside, the maintenance of contact with the outside world with especial reference to the prisoner's family and his prospects of employment on release, another task which is likely to increase rather than decrease in magnitude. What I have just said should be enough to suggest that there ought always to be a plenitude of properly paid probation officers with a work schedule proportionate to the demands made upon them by their manifold duties. Accordingly, I find it most distressing to have to report to the shade of Emma Hamlyn that English probation officers are worse paid and more overworked than their counterparts in many other parts of the world. One of their number found it necessary to do two hours' work each morning as an office cleaner in order to convert his salary from the state amounting to £22 net per week into £26.[37] Improvements have been agreed, and, after ten years' service, a probation officer may now look forward to a maximum salary of £2,150 a year [38]; but it would be idle to pretend that the future glistens with the prospect either of good pay or of a sufficiently limited quantity of work to be compatible with efficiency.

Yet this is not all. Whenever further alternatives to

---

[36] p. 82, *supra*.
[37] See the article by Peter Evans, *The Times*, May 4, 1971.
[38] *The Times*, August 7, 1971.

imprisonment are under consideration, further demands on the probation and after-care service are pretty sure to be in the background. When, in the autumn of 1970, the report of the Advisory Council on Non-custodial Penalties recommended that the courts should have power to order an offender to perform a specified number of hours' service to the community in his spare time, it was also recommended that the administration of this scheme should be entrusted to the probation and after-care service. The report also recommended that the courts should have power to defer sentence for a maximum period of six months in order, for example, to see what steps the offender took with regard to restitution, and added that the probation and after-care service would, in general, be the most suitable body to furnish the court with the necessary report when the offender reappeared for sentence. Further recommendations were that the courts should be empowered to combine a fine or suspended sentence with a probation order; if these recommendations are adopted there will of course again be more work for the probation officer.

Even this is not all, for we constantly hear suggestions that the report to which I have just referred does not go far enough, and we shall see that most of the further proposals which are remotely viable involve demands on the probation and after-care service. A recruiting campaign is clearly called for; it should include a call for more salaried staff and volunteers to aid the probation officer with part of his work, and the possibility of employing or enlisting the aid of ex-prisoners should not be ignored.

Suspended prison sentences. " The suspended sentence is wrong in principle and to a large extent impracticable.

It should not be adopted either in connection with probation or otherwise." Thus spoke the Advisory Council on the Treatment of Offenders in 1952.[39] Nevertheless the suspended prison sentence was introduced into English law by the Criminal Justice Act 1967, though not in connection with probation. If the council was right in 1952, nothing that occurred between that date and 1967 rendered its words less telling; but was the council right?

A suspended sentence differs from a conditional discharge because the offender is made fully aware, at the time of his conviction of the offence in respect of which it is imposed, of the precise nature of the sword of Damocles which will descend upon him if he commits another offence during the period of suspension which may be from one to three years. In the case of a conditional discharge, the offender only knows that, in the event of his reconviction during the period of the discharge, the maximum extent of which may again be three years, he is liable to be punished for his former offence. Advocates of the suspended sentence take the view that there are offenders who benefit from the more specific knowledge. The council did not share this view but, although they expressed their dissent in Latin, " *omne ignotum pro magnifico*," it is difficult to see how any question of principle arises. The impracticability of the suspended sentence was thought to be due to the difficulty of ensuring that it was not automatically made operative by a conviction for a venial offence during the period of suspension. This has been adequately met by the provision that the court convicting for the second offence need not bring the suspended sentence fully into force or at all if, by reason of facts occurring

[39] The report is reprinted as App. D. to the Council's report on alternatives to short terms of imprisonment published in 1957.

after the first conviction (including those of the later offence), it is thought to be unjust to do so.[40]

It seems therefore that the Advisory Council was wrong in 1952; but, before hastening to this conclusion, it is important to bear in mind that there are two schools of thought with regard to adding to the number of penal measures available to the courts. According to one school, this should only be done if obvious advantages will follow; according to the other school, the greater the number of available measures, the more are we likely to learn about the control of crime. I confess to membership of the second school, but members of the first school may well feel justified in pointing a triumphant finger at what has happened in the case of the suspended sentence.

It was intended to take the place of imprisonment, especially in the case of an offender with regard to whom all other measures short of imprisonment had failed in the past or were inappropriate having regard to the gravity of the current offence. There is, however, incontrovertible evidence that suspended sentences have been imposed in cases in which the offender would formerly have been fined and, to a lesser extent, where he would formerly have been put on probation. This much appears from an important article by Dr. Sparks of the Cambridge Institute of Criminology.[41] The author also makes the interesting point that these occurrences were largely to be expected because it was common for magistrates, having reached the conclusion that the offender ought to be in prison, to give him a last chance by imposing a fine.

Early in 1969 the Court of Appeal expressed itself as follows:

40 Criminal Justice Act 1967, s. 40 (1).
41 [1971] Crim.L.R. 384.

" It seems to the Court that before one gets to a suspended sentence at all, the court must go through the process of eliminating other possible courses such as absolute discharge, conditional discharge, probation order, fines, and then say to itself: this is a case for imprisonment, and the final question, it being a case for imprisonment, is immediate imprisonment required or can I give a suspended sentence? " [42]

No doubt the courts pay heed to these words but Dr. Sparks estimates that a quarter of those receiving suspended sentences in 1969 would have been fined before the suspended sentence became available. The great damage caused by giving a suspended sentence in these cases is of course due to the fact that, on reconviction, the offender is likely to find himself in prison for a longer time than would formerly have been the case, *viz.* for the period of his suspended sentence, plus such further period as is imposed for the next offence. Moreover, it is difficult to escape the conclusion that the existence of the suspended sentence enhances the offender's chances of imprisonment for a subsequent offence. The overall result has been an increase in the prison population after an initial decrease in the year 1969.

It would be utterly wrong to draw any firm conclusions about the merits of the suspended sentence until we have had further experience, if only because we shall not be able to estimate its success rate for several years to come. What we want to know is the number of people who received suspended sentences in 1968, 1969 and 1970 who went through the period of suspension without a further conviction. Properly administered, the suspended sentence may yet prove to have

[42] *Per* Lord Parker C.J. in *R.* v. *O'Keefe* [1969] 1 All E.R. 526.

been the means of keeping some offenders out of prison by having shown them the red light at the right moment. According to the Prison Department's report of 1970 about 60 per cent. of those receiving suspended sentences will not, on present trends, be convicted during the period of suspension.

The wait and see policy which I have just canvassed does not mean that there should be no legislation in the meantime. The obligation, subject to important exceptions, to suspend sentences of six months or less on persons who have not previously been in prison, is frowned on in some quarters. Perhaps it should be abolished in favour of a provision that courts must always give reasons for not suspending a sentence of less than two years, or that they should always do so in the case of the first prison sentence. Two years is the maximum sentence which can be suspended. I do not suggest that it should be enlarged, although such a suggestion is sometimes made. A suspended sentence of ten years has even been proposed as the last desperate measure to stop a recidivist in full career, and I cannot say that I regard the suggestion as any worse for having come from a persistent false pretender.[43]

Offenders under twenty-one. Children under fourteen were rendered immune from imprisonment by the Children Act of 1908. The tendency of subsequent legislation has been to render this class of offender totally immune from judicial punishment. The age of criminal responsibility at common law was seven. It was raised to eight by the Children and Young Persons Act 1933 as a result of one

[43] One of the inmates of Grendon Underwood mentioned in *The Frying Pan* by Tony Parker, p. 205.

of the dampest squibs that can ever have been set off by
fiery words:

> " The age of 7 was adopted hundreds of years ago and
> the whole attitude of society towards offences committed
> by children has since been *revolutionised*. We think the
> time has come for raising the age of criminal responsi-
> bility, and we think it could *safely* be placed at 8." [44]

The age of criminal responsibility was raised to ten by the
Children and Young Persons Act 1963, thanks to the action
in the House of Lords of a very distinguished Hamlyn lecturer.[45] If Part I of the Children and Young Persons Act
1969 is ever brought fully into force, homicide will be the
only offence for which a child under fourteen can be prose-
cuted. This may well be the position before the end of the
present Parliament so far as a child between the ages of
ten and twelve is concerned.

Does this mean that, homicide apart, the age of criminal
responsibility will have been raised to fourteen when the
Act of 1969 is fully operative? The answer to this conundrum
is,

> " No, because in the case of a child between the ages
> of 10 and 14, the issue of his criminal responsibility will
> still have to be determined, by the standard of proof
> appropriate to criminal cases, in care proceedings."

Under section 1 (2) of the Act, an order (including a care or
supervision order) may be made if, *inter alia*, the child is
guilty of an offence, excluding homicide, and he is also in
need of care or control which he is unlikely to receive unless

---

[44] Report of the Committee on the Treatment of Young Offenders (1927)
Cmd. 2831, p. 21.
[45] Lady Wootton.

the court makes an order. The effect of section 3 (3) is that the court cannot find that the child has committed an offence unless it would have found him guilty of the offence before the Act. This leaves us with the common law, warts and all, and there are two warts which ought to have been removed while the going was good, although I am not suggesting that they do much harm.

The first is the rebuttable presumption of innocence according to which a child under fourteen cannot be found guilty of an offence unless the prosecution proves that he knew that his conduct was gravely wrong. In practice, very little reliance seems to be placed on the presumption, but, in theory, it could produce absurd results. For example, the court may entertain no doubt (a) that a child of ten-and-a-half broke into an empty house and stole from it, and (b) that he is in need of care or control which he is unlikely to receive unless it makes an order; yet it may be unable to do this for want of proof that the child knew that burglary of empty houses is gravely wrong. Of course the burglary may be treated as evidence that the child is in moral danger, or beyond the control of his parents; in either of these events an order could be made, but a good deal more evidence than the burglary would be required.

The second wart is the conclusive presumption that a boy under fourteen is incapable of sexual intercourse. As to this, let it suffice for me to quote for your derision the only attempt to justify the presumption that I have ever come across. It comes from Bishop, the great nineteenth century American expositor of the criminal law; and it has even received judicial approval, but only in New South Wales in the early days when the judges were confronted with the argument that the presumption was unsuited to the local climate.

> "We can hardly suppose the instances of physical capability exhibited at an earlier age in a boy sufficiently numerous to call for the abolition of a technical rule so well adapted as this to prevent those particular statements of indecent things which wear away the nice sense of the refined, placed by the Maker, in the human mind as one of the protections of its virtue." [46]

Although the Act of 1969 does not raise the age of criminal responsibility, it will, when fully in force, preclude every kind of criminal prosecution of a child under fourteen except one for homicide. The exception is presumably intended to allow for the public concern which might be occasioned by some homicides by children.[47] Anyone disposed to lament the total disappearance of the possibility of punishment in all other cases, should pause to reflect on the insignificance of the loss. It will mean that a child under fourteen convicted on indictment of an offence punishable with imprisonment of fourteen years or more can no longer be detained as directed by the Home Secretary for the period specified by the court under section 53 (2) of the Children and Young Persons Act 1933; this is something which hardly ever happens now.[48] It will mean that a child under

[46] *R.* v. *Willis* (1865) 4 S.C.R. 59.
[47] Under s. 53 (1) of the Children and Young Persons Act 1933 a child or young person convicted of murder must be detained at Her Majesty's pleasure in such place as the Home Secretary may direct. Under s. 53 (2) a child or young person may be detained in such a place for the period specified by the court on conviction of an offence punishable with fourteen years imprisonment or more. So far as a child is concerned, s. 53 (2) will only apply to manslaughter when the Act of 1969 is fully operative.
[48] There was one case in 1968, none in 1969 and none in 1970.

fourteen can no longer be fined, and that a boy can no longer be directed to attend an attendance centre over successive weekends, generally for periods of two hours, up to a maximum of twelve. Surely it is not worth making much of a song and dance about the loss of a power to impose a fine which is usually paid by the parents, or the loss of the power to make a delinquent boy who, *ex hypothesi,* is not in need of care or control to such an extent as to render a court order desirable, attend a police station, school or youth club for some Saturday P.T., craft instruction or improving discourse. The truth is that judicial punishment is too blunt an instrument for children under fourteen. In their case the proper function of the court is to act as last resort decision-maker in cases in which it proves to be impossible for satisfactory arrangements to be made between parents and the local authority; this is what is secured by the provisions of the Act of 1969 with regard to care proceedings.

That Act will, if and when it is fully operative, reduce the liability of young persons between the ages of fourteen and seventeen to punishment. They secured complete immunity from imprisonment in consequence of the Criminal Justice Act 1961, but several other penal measures are still available against them. If convicted on indictment of homicide or any offence punishable with fourteen years imprisonment or more, they may be detained under section 53 of the Children and Young Persons Act 1933, and this power will be retained by the court even when the Act of 1969 is fully operative. This will also be true of the present power to fine a young person, but the courts' power to send a boy between the ages of fourteen and seventeen to a junior detention centre, or to order his attendance at an attendance centre, or to send a young person of either sex who is above the age of fifteen to Borstal will have disappeared. Moreover, it will only be possible to prosecute young persons for offences falling within categories to be specified by the Home Secretary. These will include offences of a serious nature or of considerable public concern.

The court will continue to have power to make a super-vision or care order, and it may well prove to be the case that a young person subject to such an order can be directed to reside for a while in a place bearing a striking resemblance to a junior detention centre, or to attend periodically at a place very like an attendance centre. It remains to be seen whether the gigantic reorganisation at present being under-taken by the local authorities which will result in a system of community homes and places for intermediate treatment will produce more than a change in name of corrective measures. This observation must not be taken to imply disapproval of the Act of 1969 for it is based on three assumptions which seem to me to be very sensible. These are first, that the needs of a delinquent child or young per-son are similar to those of his neglected brothers and that this is especially true in the case of the child; second, that juvenile court is *functus officio* once it has decided that a child or young person should be placed in care, with the result that the local authority is *in loco parentis*, or under the supervision of the local authority acting through its children's officer, in which case the right of parental control remains. Third, that the delinquent children require treat-ment to the exclusion of punishment, while delinquent young persons usually require treatment rather than judicial punish-ment. I find it hard to believe that the most ardent advocate of punishment would want to man the barricades in order to preserve the junior detention centre or to enable boys and girls of fifteen to be sent to Borstal. However, it would be idle to deny that the Act has its enemies, and there will certainly be no undue haste on the part of the present government in bringing it fully into operation.

The scheme for offenders in the seventeen to twenty-one age group adumbrated in Penal Practice in a Changing Society and implemented by the Criminal Justice Act 1961 will, if it becomes fully operative (a most unlikely contingency), render members of the group immune from imprisonment for periods of less than three years. The scheme is that, where a custodial sentence of six months or less is deemed proper, the offender should be sent to a detention centre; where a custodial sentence of from six months to two years is deemed proper, an order for Borstal training should be made; and the offender should only be sent to prison for periods of three years or more. The scheme has not been brought into full operation because there are not enough detention centres to enable prisons to be replaced by them when a court proposes to pass a custodial sentence of six months or less.

The treatment of the seventeen to twenty-one age group is at present under consideration by the Advisory Council on the Penal System. This in itself may be thought sufficient to justify my reference to the complete implementation of the scheme of the White Paper as a most unlikely contingency, but there is a further reason, namely, the great unpopularity among the judges of section 3 (1) of the Criminal Justice Act 1961 which embodies the main part of the scheme and is very much in operation. It reads as follows:

" Without prejudice to any other enactment prohibiting or restricting the imposition of imprisonment on persons of any age, sentence of imprisonment shall not be passed by any court on a person within the limits of age which qualify for a sentence of Borstal training except —(a) for a term not exceeding six months; or (b) (where the court has power to pass such a sentence) for a term of not less than three years."

The present age limits for Borstal are fifteen to twenty-one, and the permissible period of custody in a Borstal institution is from six months to two years. Within those limits, the offender may be released on licence at any time.

The judges tend to dislike fetters on their sentencing powers such as that contained in section 3 (1) of the Criminal Justice Act 1961, and I think that most people would agree that experience has shown that the subsection can produce absurd results. It led to two Cambridge undergraduates who, in the opinion of the trial judge and Court of Appeal, merited a year's imprisonment as punishment for a riot, finishing up with sentences of Borstal training.[49] After observing incidentally that section 3 (1) is said to work to the detriment of Borstal institutions in that they have to receive all and sundry instead of those assessed by the courts as being suitable, Sachs L.J. speaking for the Court of Appeal, said: " It is also plain that in practice no one sentenced to Borstal training is likely to suffer with regard to the overall length of a custodial sentence." But the fact remains that someone sentenced to Borstal training is on risk for a longer period of incarceration than someone sentenced to a year's imprisonment. The risk decreases more or less daily with the decline, due to the increased demand for places, in the average custodial period of a Borstal sentence; but, even at the 1970 rate, while the offender sentenced to

[49] *R.* v. *Caird and Others* (1970) 54 Cr.App.R. 499, p. 509.

a year's imprisonment would be released on remission after eight months, the average period of custody for a Borstal trainee was thirty-seven weeks plus the time spent in an allocation centre.[50]

I am reminded of an occasion when I gave a talk to schoolboys and schoolgirls who were contemplating reading law at Oxford. When the time for questions came, a girl confronted me with a horrible poser: " If we are now adults when we are eighteen, why can we still be sent to Borstal? " I reacted with a hastily contrived and somewhat self-contradictory statement about Borstal being more agreeable than prison and how training takes a long time; for good measure I threw in the remarks of Sachs L.J. which I have just quoted. But my questioner seemed to remain unconvinced and murmured something which I did not catch about allocation centres. She was evidently well on the way to being a first class student of penology.

Once again we are faced with the problem raised by Professor Norval Morris: should we always act on the principle that the maximum of a man's punishment should never be greater than the amount which would be justified by other aims of our criminal justice than that of reform.[51] For my own part, I am content to treat the principle as nothing more than a strong presumption and to reply " Only if the additional period is not excessively long, and provided there is clear evidence that it will generally have beneficial consequences." As I have already indicated, it seems to me that the evidence is not sufficiently clear to warrant the addition of a day to

[50] Report of the Prison Department for 1970, para. 29. The Home Secretary has power to release on licence in special cases within a period of less than six months.
[51] p. 56 and p. 102, *supra.*

a prison sentence in the name of reform, and I am bound to say that the recent decline in the Borstal success rate makes me equally sceptical about the consequences of Borstal training.[52] Why not let offenders of eighteen and over receive custodial sentences of the same length as the courts would mete out in the case of ordinary imprisonment, due allowance being made, in appropriate cases, for the offender's youth? Let the Executive decide on the type of regime under which the period in custody should be spent, and why not give the Executive power to release the offender on licence whenever it thinks fit to do so? These highly indefinite sentences could be introduced, in the first instance, for the seventeen to twenty-one age group in place of the present system, involving detention centres, Borstal and imprisonment; I have a feeling that it would be gradually extended to all age groups.

I do not want anything that I have said to imply that we can give up all attempts to train offenders in the seventeen to twenty-one age group. I am only saying that it is wrong to keep them in custody longer than would otherwise be the case for the sake of training. Subject to this reservation, I am all in favour of the most positive efforts at reclamation. The offender is in one of the most trainable age groups and, what is often overlooked, he is in an age group upon which incarceration can all too easily have the most deformatory effect. Boredom and membership of a sub-culture may well have got him into trouble, he is only likely to be redeemed by having his interests aroused and by finding something interesting to do on release. The achievement of this state of affairs is, needless to say, something

[52] p. 133, *infra*.

which is easier said than done. Let us look at the way we try to do it.

Senior detention centres. Detention centres were introduced into the English penal system by the Criminal Justice Act 1948 in response to a need, voiced as far back as 1927 [53] for " some form of short detention in an establishment other than a prison for a maximum period of six months." It was said that such establishments could either be regarded as short term Borstal institutions or as separate prisons for persons under twenty-one. The proposal did not find favour with the 1927 Committee on the Treatment of Young Offenders because it did not allow sufficient time for training; but faith in the curative effects of long term incarceration of the young had begun to dwindle, even by 1948. In a sense the pendulum had swung to the opposite extreme, for detention centres had come to be thought of as places where the young offender in need of discipline would receive a short sharp shock. By 1970, however, the Advisory Council on the Penal System had come to the conclusion that " . . . the punitive function of detention in a detention centre should be regarded as fulfilled by the deprivation of the offender's liberty." Their report added that treatment within the centre should be aimed at bringing about a change in the offender's behaviour.[54] The type of regime by which it was sought to bring about this change, before effect was given to the council's recommendations, is best described in the words of one of the inmates of the senior detention centre at Whatton, near Nottingham, whose essay was kindly procured for me by the Warden, Mr. W. R. Ritson. It will be found

[53] Report of the Committee on the Treatment of Young Offenders, p. 87.
[54] Report on Detention Centres, para. 63.

in the Appendix to this lecture. In consequence of the recommendation it is likely that less attention will be paid to factory style work and more to farming; while contacts between the centres and the community will be encouraged.

The most usual detention centre order is for a period of three months, but, under section 4 of the Criminal Justice Act 1961, an order may be made committing the offender to a detention centre for a period of from three to six months, provided he has attained the age of seventeen and his offence is punishable with a maximum of more than three months imprisonment. Boys from fourteen to seventeen may still be sent to junior detention centres where they will receive full time education up to school-leaving age, although, as we have seen, these centres will cease to exist as such if ever the Children and Young Persons Act 1969 becomes fully operative. The one detention centre for junior and senior girls has been discontinued. Release is on licence for a year, following remission of a third of the sentence.

Assessments of the merits of detention centres vary slightly, but I am prepared to accept the verdict of the Advisory Council's report after a consideration of the relevant research studies.

" The deduction that we draw from these studies is that, for young men with not very serious criminal careers, detention in a detention centre is as effective as short term imprisonment, and possibly as effective as the longer term Borstal training ."[55]

The reconviction rate on a follow-up of three years was said to be more than 50 per cent.[56]

[55] *Ibid.* para. 61.
[56] *Ibid.* para. 51.

Borstal.   Borstal used to be regarded as one of the greatest achiements of the English penal system.   Paterson raved about it, and Ruggles-Brise was only slightly less enthusiastic.   Estimates of its merits have become deflated with the decline in its success rate, but it would be wrong not to make some reference to the history and heyday of Borstal.

After stating that the majority of habitual criminals are made between the ages of sixteen and twenty-one, paragraph 84 of the Gladstone Report did recommend, as an experiment, the establishment of a penal reformatory under government management.

> " It should be begun on a moderate scale, but on a design which would allow of larger expansion if the results were proved to be satisfactory.   The court should have power to commit to these establishments offenders under the age of twenty-three for periods of not less than one year and up to three years, with a system of licences graduated according to sentence, which should be freely exercised."

The result, after some trifling experimentation in Bedford Prison, was the utilisation of a wing of the convict prison at Borstal, near Rochester, for the detention of " juvenile-adult " prisoners under a special regime.   This included " strict disciplinary rules, some instruction in trades, basic education and a system of grades through which the inmates gained promotion and increasingly small privileges by earning marks for hard work and good conduct."[57]

The experiment was sufficiently successful to warrant the enactment of Part I of the Prevention of Crime Act 1908.   It

[57] R. Hood, *Borstal Reassessed*, p. 15.   I am heavily indebted to this admirable book.

authorised Assizes and Quarter Sessions to pass, in lieu of a sentence of penal servitude or imprisonment, a sentence of detention " under penal discipline in a Borstal institution for a term of not less than one year nor more than three years." The offender upon whom such a sentence might be passed had to be between the ages of sixteen and twenty-one, and it had to appear to the court that:

> " by reason of his criminal habits and tendencies, or associations with persons of bad character, it is expedient that he should be subject to detention for such term and under such instruction and discipline as appears most conducive to his reformation and the repression of crime."

" Borstal institutions " were defined by section 4 (1) as places in which young offenders might be given " such industrial training and other instruction, and be subjected to such disciplinary and moral influences as will conduce to their reformation and the prevention of crime." Release on licence could take place at any time after six months, and the licence was to last for six months. There have been subsequent variations in the age limits, the maximum and minimum permissible periods of custody, and in the duration of the licence. Under the Criminal Justice Act 1961, anyone between fifteen and twenty-one can be sentenced to Borstal training. No period is specified by the court, but the maximum that may be spent in custody is two years, the minimum (subject to a special order by the Home Secretary) six months; release is on licence which may be of two years' duration. As we have seen, the minimum age limit will be raised to seventeen, if and when the Children and Young Persons Act 1969 is fully effective.

The regime of disciplinary rules, some instruction in trades, basic education and a system of grades was maintained throughout Ruggles-Brise's chairmanship of the Prison Commission. The following time table for males is taken from the Appendix to his book, *The English Prison System*:

5.40 a.m.	Inmates rise.
6.15 ,,	Drill.
6.45 ,,	Inmates' breakfast.
7.30 ,,	Chapel.
8.0 a.m.	Labour.
12 noon	Inmates' dinner.
1.0 p.m.	Labour.
5.0 ,,	Inmates' tea.
5.40 ,,	Evening School, Silent hour and recreation.
8.30 ,,	Inmates locked up.

One can but be struck by its similarity to that of the regime of today, as portrayed by an inmate of the Huntercombe Borstal. His account, kindly procured by Mr. Adrian Arnold, governor of Huntercombe, will be found in the Appendix to this lecture.

It is commonly said that the regime suffered from being para-military in the days of Ruggles-Brise and that Patterson re-modelled Borstal on something approximating to public school lines. Indeed, Paterson himself may have done something to foster this belief, for he appears to have told his friend and admirer, Barclay Barron, that he found Borstal " little more than a boys' prison, as nearly akin to a prison as dog racing is to horse racing," and re-founded it on educational lines.[58] No doubt there was more relaxation,

[58] *Toc H Journal*, January 1948. Correspondence in the possession of John Murray & Co. which Mr. Murray has kindly allowed me to see

more experimentation and a thorough development of the house system in Paterson's day; but there were more Borstals in which these things could be done, and, on the whole, a more sympathetic public. The instructions in the Appendix to Ruggles-Brise's book rather give the lie to the para-military notion and this is what he said about them:

"The 'tutors' are a special feature of the institutions. They are in a sense house masters, or masters of sections or wings of inmates. They are selected for their special qualifications for dealing with lads of this age and character, each of whom it is their duty to 'individualise,' *i.e.* to observe closely."[59]

Even the open Bostal for which so much credit is given to Paterson [60] was mooted in the days of Ruggles-Brise, and the idea might have come to fruition but for the 1914 war.[61]

However, it is Paterson who has immortalised Borstal of the 1930s with a plethora of his aphorisms and clichés, call them what you will.

"Borstal training is based on the double assumption that there is individual good in each, and among nearly all an innate corporate spirit, which will respond to the appeal made to the British of every sort, to play the game, to follow the flag, to stand by the old ship." [62]

I have no wish to deny the truth of this statement, but it makes me feel sick, and I have often asked myself why this

shows that Paterson, albeit rather reluctantly, approved of the description of Borstal as "not a bad public school" in the Appendix to Shane Leslie's biography of Sir Evelyn Ruggles-Brise.

[59] *The English Prison System*, p. 98.
[60] p. 32, *supra*.   [61] Hood, *op. cit.* p. 31.
[62] *The Principles of the Borstal System*, p. 8. Paterson's authorship of this pamphlet published by the Prison Commissioners in 1932, has, so far as I am aware, never been doubted.

should be so. The answer is that I regard the remark, in its context, as one of the most pernicious manifestations of the disease of " PLU " (people like us).

No doubt we have all frequently felt that the world would be a better place if only it were inhabited by people like us, but it seems to me that the English penal system in particular has been bedevilled by the confidence displayed by high minded people in the belief that the right way to treat a low-minded criminal is to deal with him as they would like to be dealt with if they had committed a crime. Paterson's words were written as an introduction to a thorough canvassing of the merits of inculcating middle class values, derived from the public school, in the minds of Borstal boys. Of the same ilk was the confidence displayed in the eighteenth century by Howard and others in a protracted version of the solitary confinement of the Easter retreat as a cure for crime. It is even possible that the same criticism may be validly advanced against the contemporary view that it is imperative that we should provide prisoners with a regular day's compulsory work, and most regrettable that we are generally unable to do so.

But I must not allow my distaste for his words to prevent me from doing Paterson and his admirable appointees full honour for their achievement with regard to Borstal. Borstal *was* a success in the late 1930s. Well-authenticated figures show a success rate of around 60 per cent. after a three year follow-up. At Lowdham Grange, the first open Borstal, which was, in a sense, the apple of Patterson's eye, it was as high as 77 per cent. An overall success rate of 73 per cent. had been claimed by Ruggles-Brise who tells us that statistics published shortly before the 1914 war concerning 1,454 cases discharged on licence since the Act of 1908 came into force, show that only 392, or 27 per cent. had been reconvicted [63]; but these figures are suspect.[64]   Since the war there has been steady deterioration.   By 1970 the success rate was down to 30 per cent. on a three year follow-up.[65]

What accounts for this?   One very plausible suggestion is the change in the type of boy who finds his way to Borstal.   To quote from the Prison Commissioners' report of 1957:

> " Lads now coming in Borstal do not speak the same kind of language as the staff.   They are now so often coming from a background that has a different type of mental outlook.   When we discuss matters of ethics, dishonesty, deceit, lying and such like and show we consider them to have wrong standards, we are looked upon as not being part of this world."

In 1952 under one in eight Borstal boys had more than six previous convictions or findings of guilt, in 1962 one in two came into this category.[66]   An increasing number of inmates have had previous institutional treatment at an approved school, detention centre or prison.   Other possible, though unproved, reasons for the decline in the Borstal success rate are the shortening of the period spent in custody which has been due to overcrowding rather than any shift in penological opinion, and the fact that, since the Criminal Justice Act 1961 came into force, the courts have had to send all young offenders thought to deserve custodial treatment of more than six months and less than three years to Borstal.

Whatever be the cause, the experiment of reclaiming

---

[63] *The English Prison System*, p. 95.
[64] Hood, *op. cit.* p. 206.
[65] Report of the Prison Department, para. 60.
[66] Hood, *op. cit.* pp. 153–154.

delinquent youth by instruction in the values of the play-
ground and incarceration in houses on the public school
model with appeals to follow the flag has been a failure with
the post-war generations. There is no doubt that it is being
replaced by something else,[67] but it is exceedingly difficult
to get a clear picture of what that something else is. Hostels
and work in the community with the sanction of incarceration in a very closed Borstal may be the ultimate answer in
many, but certainly not in all, cases.

Mentally abnormal offenders. One of the sticks with
which the Rev. W. D. Morrison was wont to beat the Du
Cane regime was the assertion that, thanks to the prevailing
prison conditions, insanity was rife in our prisons. This
allegation was considered by the Gladstone Committee which
inclined to the view that the disproportionately large number
of insane and feeble-minded people in the prison population
was due to the fact that a disproportionately large number
of prisoners were insane or feeble-minded on reception. The
committee's report recommended that candidates for medical
appointments in prison should be required to show that they
had given special attention to lunacy, that weak-minded
prisoners should be concentrated, so far as possible, in a
special prison, and that " it should be considered whether
it is right to treat such persons as ordinary criminals."

" They cannot be said to be fully responsible for their
actions, and when they take to crime it would be better
for them and for the community that they should be
sent to some special institution in the nature of an
asylum, where they might do light work under detention,

[67] B. S. Alper, 8 *British Journal of Criminology*, p. 6.

the period of which might vary according to their physical and mental condition." [68]

So far as the last recommendation was concerned, the committee had, in a sense, been anticipated by a Home Office circular of 1889 in which magistrates were instructed to dismiss the less serious cases involving a weak-minded offender, handing him over to friends or causing him to be sent to an asylum. This is not the place in which to enlarge on the development of the law and practice with regard to the mentally ill offender in the twentieth century. I renounce the duty all the more enthusiastically on account of my fore-knowledge of the contents of Chapter 17 of Volume II of Dr. Walker's *Crime and Insanity* in England to be published shortly. You will find there as comprehensive an account as you need ask for of the work of the Royal Commission on the Care and Control of the Feeble-minded, presided over by Lord Radnor between 1905 and 1908, the Mental Deficiency Acts of 1913 and 1927, the relevant provisions of the Criminal Justice Act 1948 and the work of the Royal Commission on the Law relating to Mental Illness and Mental Deficiency presided over by Lord Percy from 1954 to 1958. The Criminal Justice Act 1948 empowers the courts to make probation orders subject to a condition of psychiatric treatment, and the Mental Health Act 1959 empowers the courts to make hospital or guardianship orders in the case of someone convicted of any offence punishable with imprisonment other than treason or murder, provided the prescribed medical evidence is forthcoming. The effect of a hospital order is that the offender is committed to a mental hospital until cured in which case he must be released; but

[68] Paras. 92–93.

the order may be made subject to restriction for a fixed or indefinite period, in which case the offender cannot be released during the currency of the restriction without the consent of the Home Secretary.

Although there is no doubt a large class of mentally ill offenders who would rather be in a prison than a mental hospital, if only on account of their horror of being thought " nuts," I do not think anyone would wish to quarrel with the developments to which I have referred. Prison is no place for the mentally ill. Accordingly I can but lament the acceptance by the courts of the view that, even in cases in which a hospital order could be made, it is perfectly proper for a judge to take the view that punishment is required and, *on that ground*, sentence the offender to imprisonment. I am not for one moment quarrelling with the course, sometimes adopted by the courts, of sentencing a dangerous offender to imprisonment for life on the ground that there is no available accommodation in a sufficiently secure mental hospital, or even (though I confess to reservations here) on the ground that it would be preferable for the Home Secretary to transfer the offender to a mental hospital, so that, in the interests of security, he could be returned to prison for observation before release when cured.[69] What I do say is that the punishment of the seriously mentally ill is theoretically indefensible, and that this is so whether or not the offender's responsibility was impaired at the time of the act or omission in respect of which he is charged. Punishing the mentally ill is just as indefensible as flogging the physically deformed.

Perhaps the gross impropriety of punishing the mentally ill is rendered less obvious by the fact that one of the leading

[69] *R.* v. *Harvey and Ryan*, unreported, July 16, 1971.

cases concerned a finding of diminished responsibility,[70] with the attendant suggestion that some reduced punishment was permissible. No account of the reduction and avoidance of punishment during the twentieth century could be really complete without a reference to the law governing this defence; but I find it convenient to defer this question to my next lecture.

On the whole, the story told in this lecture is one of progress in penal reform, but what of that " most important of all prison questions," recidivism? This is the first topic of my next and final lecture.

APPENDIX

Essay by a six-month trainee at Whatton Detention Centre—
My Detention Centre Sentence

I HAVE now one week left to do and then my four month sentence will be at an end. In a Detention Centre, one has a choice, a decision to make; either one gets on with what he has to do, and to appreciate the help that is given, or there is the other course—the one I took. I did not appreciate the help that detention was offering me. I felt disillusioned and I could not face up to what I had to do.

When I arrived at this Detention Centre at Whatton on February 23, 1971, it looked from the outside like a College, but a College with a wire fence around it. An officer opened the main door and I went in. There was a small office inside where I was told to go. Inside stood two boys and another officer, one of the boys holding a box with the number eighty-eight written on it; this was to be my property box.

70 *R.* v. *Morris* [1961] 2 Q.B. 237.

The Officer looked at me and came towards me; he searched me and what he found he put into the box.

After that I was taken to have a bath and then a medical officer examined me and told me to follow him. We went down a corridor which was dark and there were detention rooms (cells) on one side. I was put into one; there was nothing in the room except a small table and chair. I sat down and put my head in my hands and that was when I thought my world had ended. Later I was put into the hospital for not eating and for not obeying the officers. After I had been in the hospital a few days I finally came to my senses. I thought to myself, " Well I have got to do my sentence, so I'd better get on with it and do it."

I was then taken out of hospital and was put on the Unit where all the other boys were.

Thereafter I took part in the daily routine which I shall describe, except that in the afternoons and when required I became the Tutor-Organiser's orderly, assisting him. This work I thoroughly enjoyed doing because I felt trusted and useful.

After a few days on the Unit I soon got into the everyday routine. We got up in the morning at 6.30 a.m., had a wash and shave, then we made our beds and tidied our kits. An officer would then come round and inspect us, then we would go and have our breakfasts. By this time it was 7.15; breakfast finished at 8.00 a.m. and then it was time for work.

We lined up and marched to the parade square, where we lined up in our department columns. We were inspected again, counted and then marched off to either the trade departments or workshops There are four different trade training courses which you can choose from when you come to the Detention Centre. They give you a chance to learn a trade while you are here and also give you a good chance to get a stable job when you leave, which is a good advantage. The Trade Training courses are Bricklaying, Painting and Decorating, Plastering and Engineers'.

Also all the boys have one hour's P.E. each day, taken at different times.

There are workshops for the boys who do not have a Trade Training course. In these workshops they do various jobs for some big firms around Nottingham. We work in these departments until about 12.30 when we then have an hour off for our lunch. We then line up in the same manner after dinner as we do in the morning and then go back into these departments until 5.00 p.m.

Then we get washed and changed into our evening clothes, ready for our evening classes after tea. The classes are the basic subjects of education, and last from 6.00 to 7.30 each evening apart from Wednesday which is Chapel night.

We then have our supper and an hour's association. Then we go to bed at 8.30 and have our night inspection and then we can read until 10.00 p.m. when the lights are turned out.

Essay by a trainee at Huntercombe Borstal—

A Day in Borstal

5.30 I wake at the sound of the night watchman doing his rounds, unbolting doors or turning on lights, ready for the ringing of the bell and staff coming on duty, for the every morning process of unlocking our doors.

I arise from my bed, slip into my working trousers and slippers, make up my blankets into a tidy box, sweep my floor if feeling energetic just in time for my door being unlocked,[71] take my towel and soap. Then it's off to do my morning toilets.

7 o'clock bell rings for breakfast. Boots over my shoulder I sleepily trudge off to breakfast.

After breakfast the very monotonous twice a day parade, then it's off to work, arrive at work 8 o'clock to start another day of my four month plastering course. Five minutes conversation with the lads concerning the previous day's happenings or the weekend sports and film. This starts the ball rolling. A few words from our instructor and my day's work is set out for me, 10 o'clock bell rings for tea break. If fortunate enough to have saved some tobacco I have a smoke and read a few pages of my book. Ten minutes and it's back to work and before I know where I am it's time for lunch. I change out of my boots and overalls. Then it's back to the wing, this is the most important part of the day or should I say biggest event of the day. Either it puts me in a good mood for the rest of the week or else a bad mood for the rest of the day, depending on whether or not I get any mail. Ten to twelve bell rings for lunch. 1 o'clock back on parade and it's off to work to complete my day, of something that if given the chance will help me through life if given enough.

4.15 a word from the instructor and it's off with boots, on with shoes and back to the wing after cleaning my tools, of course.

After watering my plant and crossing another day off my calendar I have a wash and change ready for tea. Then

---

[71] When the essay was written, the general unlocking time was 6.15, although inmates who worked in the kitchen were let out at 5.30; the general unlocking time is now 6.45.

join the congregation round the block board at the wing centre. Then it's off to tea.

After tea it's classes until eight, when it's supper time so it's back to the wing. After supper I answer any mail I may have. Then watch Television until ten past nine which is bed time. The officer locks us away. After making my bed and saying my prayers I will start to read my book and this is when I start feeling sorry for myself.

Ten o'clock lights are out. I slowly drift into a dream concerning my previous life or my future life.

RECIDIVISM AND THE COMMON MAN

1. Recidivism

To quote paragraph 18 of the Gladstone Report once again:

> " In proportion to the spread of education, the increase of wealth, and the extension of social advantages, the retention of a compact mass of habitual criminals in our midst is a growing stain on our civilisation. In any thorough enquiry into prison treatment, the closest regard must be paid to its physical and moral effect on prisoners generally. But the number of habitual criminals in and out of prison must form one of the standards by which the system must be tested and judged. Recidivism is the most important of all prison questions, and it is the most complicated and difficult.'

ABOUT thirty-five years later, Sir Alexander Paterson felt able to begin the memorandum which he submitted to the Departmental Committee on Persistent Offenders with the assertion that " the problem of recidivism is small, diminishing, and not incapable of solution." [1] The reader of the above statements could be forgiven for inferring that great progress in the treatment of recidivism had taken place in the first quarter of the twentieth century. Nothing could be further from the truth as the excellent report of the Committee so clearly revealed when it was published in 1932. But before we dismiss Paterson with utter contempt, we would do well to remember that his memorandum was written in the period of penological optimism. He believed that there were fewer recidivists on account of improved social conditions and improved methods of dealing with

---

[1] *Paterson on Prisons* (ed. S. K. Ruck), p. 55.

young offenders. There was no lack of statistics to justify his cheerfulness. He pointed to the fact that, in 1909, there was a daily average of 2,500 recidivist inmates of convict prisons serving sentences of penal servitude, whereas, in 1929, the corresponding figure was 1,200. Lest anyone should think that this simply meant that the recidivists of yore were serving sentences of imprisonment, Paterson drew attention to the fact that the number of prisoners with previous convictions received into local prisons in 1909 was 111,000, whereas it had fallen to 27,000 by 1929. At this point one begins to call for a definition of term. What did Paterson mean by a " recidivist "?

It is plain that he included the habitual drunkard for his memorandum had previously said that:

> " Some forms of recidivism have, in the experience of our lifetime, well nigh disappeared. In 1913 the number of sentences of imprisonment for alcoholic offences was nearly 50% greater than the entire number of sentences of imprisonment for all offences in 1929."

It is equally plain that the Gladstone Committee did not include the drunks among the habitual criminals concerning whom they made the recommendation I am about to quote, and they were only considered incidentally by the Committee on Persistent Offenders of 1932. I have no wish to minimise either the reduction in offences of drunkenness which took place between 1913 and 1929, or the dimensions of the problem of alcoholism in relation to the criminal law today, but, for the purposes of the present discussion, I propose to confine the term " recidivist" to someone who is repeatedly convicted of indictable offences. Subject to that restriction, I am more than content with the definition once supplied to me on the spur of the moment by Dr. Walker, Reader in Criminology at Oxford:

> " A recidivist is the offender who neither amends his ways spontaneously, nor learns to avoid detection, and who is neither deterred by the experience of conviction, nor reformed by any of the methods in the courts' repertoire."

Even when confined to the person who commits indictable offences, it is plain that a multitude of different offenders come within the above definition of a recidivist, and it seems that failure to take due account of this fact lies at the root of the lack of success of the twentieth century legislation concerning the persistent offender.

Paragraph 85 of the Gladstone Report draws a distinction between the habitual prisoner upon whom the regime had no effect unless he was sentenced to long periods of imprisonment or penal servitude which, however, frequently made him desperate and determined not to be taken alive when again at large, and the habitual criminals not of a desperate order

> " who live by robbery and thieving and petty larceny, who run the risk of comparatively short sentences with comparative indifference. They make money rapidly by crime, they enjoy life after their fashion, and then on detection and conviction they serve their term quietly with the full determination to revert to crime when they come out. . . . When under sentence they complicate prison management, when at large they are responsible for the commission of the greater part of undetected crime; they are a nuisance to the community. To punish them for the particular offence in which they are

detected is almost useless; witnesses were almost unanimous in approving some kind of cumulative sentence; the real offence is the wilful persistence in the deliberately acquired habits of crime. We venture to offer the opinion, formed during this enquiry, that a new form of sentence should be placed at the disposal of the judges by which these offenders might be segregated for long periods of detention during which they would not be treated with the severity of first class hard labour or penal servitude, but they would be forced to work, under less onerous conditions."

When, as Home Secretary, he introduced Part II of the Prevention of Crime Act 1908, Herbert Gladstone explained it to the Commons in terms of a distinction " well known to criminologists," between habituals and professionals:

" Habituals were men who drop into crime from their surroundings or physical disability, or mental deficiency, rather from any active intention to plunder their fellow creatures or from being criminal for the sake of crime. The professionals were the men with an object, sound in mind—and in body, competent, often highly skilled, and who deliberately, with their eyes open, preferred a life of crime and knew all the tricks and turns and manoeuvres necessary for that life. It was with that class that the Bill would deal." [2]

Preventive detention. So it was for the protection of the public against the professional criminal, as defined by Lord Gladstone,[3] that the new sentence of preventive detention

[2] Ruggles-Brise, *The English Prison System*, p. 52.
[3] Herbert Gladstone became a peer in 1910.

was devised. It was not required by the insufficiency of the statutory maxima periods of penal servitude for the offence which he committed, so much as by the retributive approach consistently adopted by the courts in their sentencing practice within those maxima. However bad the offender's past record might be, the sentence for the offence in respect of which he stood convicted had to bear some relation to the gravity of that offence. For those who take fear at the very word " retributive," there is a utilitarian argument in support of the practice.

> " If a man with a bad record were liable to receive the same sentence whether he were convicted of a minor larceny or of robbery with violence, there is a danger that he might more often commit the graver offence on the principle that it is better to be hanged for a sheep than a lamb." [4]

The trouble about the policy of protecting the public against the professional criminal by depriving him of his liberty for a considerably longer period than the gravity of his current crime demands, is that it assumes that the public does not need special protection against the habitual, as defined by Gladstone, and that the public receives adequate protection against the violent recidivist by the sentences meted out for his current offence. I am not disposed to cavil at either of these assumptions, but the history of preventive detention shows that many a judge has been apt to ignore Gladstone's distinction between the habitual and the professional criminal; and the very natural demand that the public should be

[4] Report of the Committee on Persistent Offenders 1932, Cmd. 4090, para. 25.

specially protected against the violent recidivist continues to
be voiced in many quarters.

The Act of 1908 provided that, where someone who had
been convicted on indictment of a crime, admitted that he
was, or was found by the jury to be, an habitual criminal,
the court might, if it passed a sentence of penal servitude for
the crime, also pass a further sentence ordering that, on
determination of the penal servitude, he be detained for a
further period of not less than five nor more than ten years.
This further period was " preventive detention." " Crime "
was defined as any felony, plus a few further specified
offences, including false pretences. An " habitual criminal "
was defined as a " person who, since the age of sixteen, had,
on at least three occasions, been convicted of a ' crime ' and
was persistently leading a criminal or dishonest life." Before
passing a sentence of preventive detention, the court had to
be of the opinion that, by reason of his criminal habits and
mode of life, it was expedient for the protection of the public
that the offender should be kept in detention for a lengthened
period of years.

The preventive detention regime was governed by the
rules applicable to convict prisons, but they were to be subject to such modifications in the direction of a less rigorous
treatment as might be made by the Home Secretary.
Prisoners undergoing preventive detention were to be liable
to such disciplinary and reformative influences, and employed on such work as might be best fitted to make them
able and willing to earn an honest livelihood on discharge.
The Home Secretary was empowered to release a preventive
detainee on licence at any time, if satisfied that there was a
reasonable probability that he would abstain from crime, and
lead a useful and industrious life, or that he was no longer

capable of engaging in crime, or that, for any other reason, it was desirable to release him from confinement in prison. The Home Secretary was advised about releases by an advisory committee. In practice a licence was granted in "comparatively hopeful cases" after three and a half years of preventive detention, when the sentence was for five years, and after seven years when the sentence was for ten years.[5] In the best of circumstances, therefore, a sentence of three years' penal servitude followed by five years' preventive detention would have meant incarceration for five and three-quarter years, while five years' penal servitude followed by ten years' preventive detention would have entailed incarceration for ten and three-quarter years.[6] The mind begins to boggle at the thought of a sentence of seven years' penal servitude followed by ten years' preventive detention in what the Home Secretary considered to be a hopeless case.

Thus there was inaugurated what came to be known as the "double track" system of treatment of persistent offenders, punishment for the offence, to be followed by isolation for the offensiveness, *i.e.*, the danger to the public. It is easy to see now why it was doomed to failure. In practice it is impossible to draw a sufficiently sharp distinction between that part of the deprivation of liberty which is punitive, and that which is merely preventive.

> " Imagine that an offender, after having served his sentence of 10 or 15 years of penal servitude, is ordered to come before the governor of the prison. The following dialogue then takes place:
>
> " The Governor: 'Today expires the term of your

[5] *Ibid.* para. 149.
[6] A quarter of the sentence of penal servitude was remitted on licence.

punishment and considerations of justice require that you should regain your liberty.'

" When the prisoner, however, is about to depart, the governor adds: ' Oh no, you cannot leave; now we must protect society and you have to go to an institution for preventive detention.'

" Upon this the offender asks: ' What change then is there to be in my life? ' To which he will get the reply, ' Up to now you have been detained in the eastern wing of the prison; from now on you will be detained in the western wing.' " [7]

Conditions in the western wing would have to verge upon those of a two, if not a three, starred hotel to make practical sense of the theoretically impeccable double track system; that would very properly be unacceptable to Parliament, public and the prison department.

However, Ruggles-Brise did his best. Camp Hill prison in the Isle of Wight was specially built for preventive detainees, and we are told that certain privileges, such as association at meals, and in the evenings, smoking, newspapers, magazines, etc., could be earned as well as a small wage, not exceeding 3d. a day, part of which could be expended on the purchase or articles of comfort from the canteen. Special provision was also made in " parole lines " for detainees thought to be approaching fitness for release on licence.[8] The reports of the Prison Commissioners were optimistic. " So far as experience up to date shows, there

[7] Von Dohna, cited in Radzinowicz and Turner, *The Modern Approach to Criminal Law*, pp. 165–166.

[8] *The English Prison System*, p. 53. The " parole lines " were log cabins outside the prison. The underlying idea was an embryonic form of the open prison or even the hostel system.

is a reasonable chance that under the Camp Hill system the habitual criminal, however bad his record, can be successfully dealt with." [9]

Even arch Jeremiahs, Hobhouse and Brockway, were almost rhapsodic. They saw preventive detention as a reformative, and asked why it should have to be preceded by penal servitude.[10] But the 1932 Committee had the last word on this subject, " All save a small proportion of these men are reconvicted after brief intervals of liberty." [11] Preventive detention was not even a deterrent, let alone a reformative. I need not remind you that the privileges which have just been mentioned have been part and parcel of ordinary prison life for ages.

At the time the Act of 1908 was passed, there was apprehension in many quarters that there would be too many sentences of preventive detention, and it was provided that the consent of the Director of Public Prosecutions had to be obtained before anyone could be charged with being an habitual criminal; but the apprehension proved to be groundless. The Departmental Committee's Report of 1932 pointed out that, between August 1909 and the end of December 1930, only 967 sentences of preventive detention had been passed in England and Wales and that, in the last ten years, the annual average had been thirty-six cases, an utterly insignificant figure when compared with the number of persons eligible. The Committee considered that the true reason why the Act had become a dead letter was that the sentence of preventive detention had to follow on one of penal servitude, and sentences of penal servitude, even for the offences which professional criminals were wont to com-

[9] Prison Commissioners' Report 1919, p. 15.
[10] *English Prisons Today*, Chap. 27.   [11] Cmd. 4090, para. 142.

mit, had become rarer than they were in 1908.[12] No doubt
this was an important point, but I think that more allowance
should be made than is customarily the case for the distaste
of the police for seeking the Directors' consent to bring the
charge of habitual criminality, of the Director for consenting,
of the jury for convicting on the charge, and of the judges
for passing a sentence of preventive detention. The double
track system was the harsh product of the purist's distinction
between punishment and detention; it could only be justified
if it really did protect the public from highly dangerous
criminals.

So what was to be said of the few offenders it did catch?
In paragraphs 137 and 138 of the Report of the Committee of
1932 they were spoken of as follows:

> " None of them is young, half of them are over fifty
> years of age, and nearly a fifth are over sixty. With
> few exceptions they are men with little mental capacity
> or strength of character. Some of them may be skilled
> in the arts of forgery or false pretences, many are
> cunning, and most of them have a strong belief in their
> own cleverness, but generally they are of the type whose
> frequent convictions testify as much to their clumsiness
> as to their persistence in crime."

In short, they bore as much resemblance as chalk does to
cheese to the professional criminals of the Gladstone Report
who, when at large, are responsible for the greater part of
undetected crime, or to those of Herbert Gladstone's speech,
" the men with an object, sound in mind—and in body,
competent, often highly skilled."

[12] p. 108, *supra.*

The 1932 Committee recommended that the courts should be empowered to pass a sentence of prolonged detention in lieu of, but not in addition to, a sentence of imprisonment or penal servitude. The power was to be exercisable if the offender had been convicted of a " crime " after three previous convictions of crime since attaining the age of sixteen and the court was of opinion that his " criminal habits and mode of life " were such that " his detention for a lengthened period of years [was] expedient for the protection of the public." " Crime " was to be defined to cover the more serious offences against property and person (including certain sexual offences); the lengthened period of detention was to be from five to ten years. The Committee had in mind criminals for whom shorter periods of detention would be inadequate either on account of the serious nature of their crimes, or else because detention for shorter periods had proved ineffective.

The ultimate and slightly modified result of the Committee's recommendations was section 21 (2) of the Criminal Justice Act 1948. I do not say " ultimate " in order to rub in the gap of sixteen years, a triviality so far as the speed of law reform is concerned, but on account of the fact that there was a Criminal Justice Bill 1938, the precursor to the somewhat different Criminal Justice Act 1948. Under section 21 (2) of the latter statute, someone over thirty convicted on indictment of an offence punishable with two years' imprisonment or more, who had previously been convicted of three such offences, and been sentenced to imprisonment, Borstal or corrective training in respect of two of them, might be sentenced to preventive detention for from five to fourteen years in lieu of any other sentence, if the court was satisfied that it was " expedient for the protection of the public that he should be detained in custody for a substantial time, followed by a period of supervision if released before the expiration of his sentence." And so, for a while, we had a single track system of special treatment for persistent offenders. Its theoretical justification depended on the drawing of a sharp distinction between imprisonment and preventive detention.

Imprisonment was to be meted out on ordinary sentencing principles. Within the permitted maximum, the length of imprisonment had to be proportionate to the gravity of the offence. Some reduction was permissible on account of such mitigating circumstances peculiar to the offender as the fact that he was exposed to temptation, or subject to exceptional pressure on account of the illness of his wife, or the breakdown of his marriage; but there could be no increase beyond the length of incarceration demanded by the gravity of the offence or, if such an increase were permitted at all, it was subject to stringent limitations on account of the impropriety of punishing twice for past offences. Such increase as was permissible on account of the offender's record could be justified both on utilitarian and retributive grounds. The utilitarian justification was simply that a little more might do the trick as a deterrent; the retributive justification was that the repetition of the offence added to its gravity on the second occasion, because the offender had deliberately flouted the law after having received the most solemn warning of the serious view taken of his conduct. (Although I have used the past tense in this brief reference to ordinary sentencing principles, I think the account holds good of today's practice.)

The length of preventive detention, as distinguished from that of imprisonment, was not to be determined by the gravity of the offence. The all-important consideration was protection of the public. *R.* v. *Caine* [13] is one of the strongest examples of the rigour with which the courts sometimes applied this doctrine. A man with fourteen previous convictions for dishonesty had been sentenced to five years' imprisonment for embezzling £21. The sentence had been imposed as the offender's last chance before he got preventive detention; but the Court of Criminal Appeal varied it to one of seven years' preventive detention because a comparatively minor offence against property did not warrant more than two years' imprisonment at the most. I wonder what Mr. Caine thought of the philosophy of the single track system.

How was preventive detention distinguished from imprisonment in practice? The sentence was divided into three stages. The first stage was no different from the lowest form of ordinary imprisonment, being spent in a local prison; the idea was to show the detainee that privileges were things to be earned, and to warn him that misbehaviour at a later stage might cause a reversion to the first. The first stage could last as long as two years, but, if all went well for nine months, the detainee would be allocated to one of the prisons which catered for those sentenced to preventive detention at which the second stage would be spent. The Prison Rules provided that a detainee who had passed into the second stage could become eligible to earn privileges over and above those allowed to a prisoner serving an ordinary sentence of imprisonment. These included slightly higher pay for work done, the cultivation of a garden and more common room association. They were more or less significant differences to begin with, but they became less and less significant as the conditions of ordinary imprisonment improved.

[13] [1963] Crim.L.R. 63.

If it was ever reached, the third stage was spent in a prison hostel. The detainee would do ordinary work outside for ordinary pay, and return to the hostel at night. Deductions were made from his wage for his keep and that of his family. All this was excellent, and, however much one ridicules the history of preventive detention, it must never be forgotten that the system gave us the pre-release hostel as we know it today; but the third stage was not often reached. An advisory board was charged with the unenviable task of deciding whether there was a reasonable probability that the offender would not revert to a criminal life, and he was only transferred to the third stage if the decision was an affirmative one. The decision was one of crucial importance to the detainees because those who were admitted to the third stage were released on licence after service of two-thirds of their sentence, while those who remained in the second stage were only released after five-sixths of the sentence had been served. According to paragraph 35 of the report of the Advisory Council on the Treatment of Offenders published on the subject of Preventive Detention in 1963, an average of no more than 27 per cent. of detainees was transferred to the third stage. The majority regarded their rejection as grossly unjust because they could not see why good behaviour throughout the second stage should not, of itself, suffice to secure promotion to the third stage. The Advisory Board's task was a well nigh impossible one, having regard to the unsatisfactory material with which it was confronted, and dissatisfaction with the stage system was one of the grounds of the Advisory Council's recommendation that section 21 (2) of the Criminal Justice Act 1948 should be repealed.

A further ground was the comparative rarity of the courts' resort to preventive detention. Paragraph 15 of the

Council's Report states that an average of about 200 offenders a year had been received under sentences of preventive detention. The paucity of such sentences had nothing to do with the lack of eligible offenders. Out of 1,384 people liable to this treatment who came before the courts in 1956, only 178 (14 per cent.) got it. One reason was no doubt the fact that many of the really serious menaces to the public were given long sentences of imprisonment for their current offences; but there seems also to be little doubt that judges flinched from imposing preventive detention for comparatively trivial offences, notwithstanding the clear distinction between the principles by which it was governed and those governing imprisonment. They knew that there was in practice no distinction between the two institutions.

Even so, an unduly large number of offenders who were, to use Herbert Gladstone's terminology, habituals rather than professionals, received sentences of preventive detention under the single track system just as they did under the double track system. To quote from an analysis by Dr. Hammond and Mrs. Chayen cited in paragraph 66 of the 1963 report of the Advisory Council,

" A third group consists of the persistent petty thief or false pretence offender who is often quite old and who has failed to make a satisfactory adjustment to life generally. He has few ties, he holds a job for a short period only, he tends to have no roots and lives from day to day in hostels, lodging houses or on the streets, and he tends to be a drain on the social services whether in prison or not. Moreover, he has been in and out of prison most of his life and appears to be better adjusted to prison life than to any other."

Extended sentences. What was thought to be wanted was something that would make it more likely that a judge would, in an appropriate case, break with the tradition of adjusting the length of a prison sentence to the gravity of the offence, and increase it disproportionately on account of the offender's record. It was believed that this could be achieved by offering the courts the opportunity of such an increase without requiring them to make the jump necessitated in the case of preventive detention. Although of opinion that two years' imprisonment was the most that could be justified by a relatively minor offence against property, a judge would be more likely, if told by a suitably worded statute that he could do so, to give up to three years, than to impose seven years' preventive detention.[14] At any rate, something like this was the object of section 37 of the Criminal Justice Act 1967.

After prohibiting any further sentences of preventive detention, it provides that, if certain conditions are fulfilled, the court may pass an extended prison sentence when satisfied that, by reason of the offender's previous conduct and of the likelihood of his committing further offences, " it is expedient to protect the public from him for a substantial time." The House of Lords has decided that the term beyond which the sentence may be extended is that which the judge would have considered appropriate to the sentence if section 37 had not been passed.[15] The extended sentence may not exceed five years if the statutory maximum for the offence is less than five years, and it may not exceed ten years if the maximum is five years or more but less than ten years. Unless he is granted parole during the second

---

[14] In practice this came to be regarded as the minimum unless the offender was very old.
[15] *Director of Public Prosecutions* v. *Ottewell* [1970] A.C. 642.

third of his sentence, a person subject to an extended sentence will be released on licence at the expiration of two-thirds of the term; in either event the licence may endure until the entire sentence expires. The conditions for an extended sentence are conviction of an offence punishable with two years' imprisonment or more, with three previous convictions on indictment for such offences. The previous offences must have been sufficiently serious to have led to substantial custodial sentences, and the current offence must have been committed within three years of the last conviction or release from custody.

Section 37 is probably better calculated to catch the professional and pass over the habitual than section 21 (2) of the Criminal Justice Act 1948; but it would be premature to make any pronouncement with regard to its use by the courts. The judges can hardly be said to have welcomed the section with open arms, for, in 1968, there were only twenty-seven extended sentences, while the numbers for 1969 and 1970 respectively were no more than seventy-four and 129.

Protection of the public. On paper section 37 of the Criminal Justice Act 1967 affords the public less chance of protection than did either section 21 (2) of the Criminal Justice Act 1948 or the Prevention of Crime Act 1908. Under section 21 (2), someone convicted of an offence, punishable with a maximum of two years' imprisonment— indecent assault upon a woman, for instance—could get up to fourteen years' preventive detention, though I very much doubt whether such a thing ever happened. Under the Act of 1908, someone convicted of a crime punishable with five years' penal servitude, say simple larceny, might have received that sentence plus a sentence of ten years' preventive detention; although I find it hard to believe that there can have been many, if any, such cases. Under the Act of 1967, the most that a suitably qualified indecent assailant of women could get would be an extended sentence of five years, and the most that a thief could get would be an extended sentence of ten years.

But I think it is important to remember that the illustrations which I have just given are largely, if not entirely, academic. Unless we are prepared to tolerate the incarceration of a certain number of people for the whole of their natural lives the protection of the public from the possible future depredations of the offender by means of a prison sentence must always be a matter of degree. The temporary incapacitation of the criminal is an element in every such sentence; the dangerous nature of an offence adds to its gravity and hence to the probable length of the sentence of those who commit it. Even when a judge is told by Parliament that he may subject a recidivist to a long period of imprisonment simply for the sake of protecting the public, he cannot wholly ignore his traditional role of the protector of the liberties of the subject (including the criminal).

At an earlier stage of this lecture, I spoke of the two assumptions underlying the policy of concentrating on the professional criminal, as pictured by the Gladstone Report and Herbert Gladstone, as the target of legislation especially concerned with persistent offenders. The first was that the public does not need special protection against the habitual; and the second assumption was that the public receives adequate protection against violent recidivists by the sentences meted out for their current offences.

I am not sure of the extent to which the distinction

between professionals and habituals would be accepted today. The habitual seems to have become the " passive inadequate deviant "; but, whatever be the name by which he goes, I do not think it is asking too much to expect the public to tolerate him. The cost of his prolonged incarceration is out of all proportion to the inconvenience caused by his depredations. In this connection it should never be forgotten that the estimated average cost of keeping a man in prison is £22 a week, as contrasted with the £1 a week of probation.[16] At the very most, let this type of offender receive the prison sentence appropriate to his current offence on ordinary sentencing principles. I say " at the very most " because I realise there is a strong argument for something like permanent probation for him, and that is a point to which I will return later. Of course it is difficult to distinguish sharply between the professional who ought to be in prison, even to the full extent of an extended sentence, and the habitual; accordingly there will continue to be some of the latter type who are receiving unnecessarily long, or even wholly unnecessary, prison sentences.

It would plainly be asking too much to expect the public to tolerate the seriously violent recidivist. Perhaps people should be more tolerant than they are of the public-house brawl or family quarrel, but the public is entitled to the fullest protection that the law can reasonably be expected to give against serious violence or serious sexual molestation. Recent research into repeated violence may be thought to have strengthened the case for a special preventive sentence for violent offenders. It shows that, in the course of a career involving recorded convictions of non-violent crime, there is

---

[16] Report of the Advisory Council on the Penal System on Non-custodial and Semi-custodial Penalties, para. 9 (1970).

a slightly increasing probability that the next conviction will be of a violent crime; but what is far more significant, the research also shows that, with each successive conviction of violence, there is a very sharply increased probability that the next conviction will be for a crime involving violence.[17] Does this mean that after, say, two convictions of violence, the court should be obliged to sentence someone convicted of further violence to a protracted period of imprisonment, say ten or even fifteen years? I have phrased the question in drastic terms so as to provoke thought on the subject. For my part, I would want clear evidence that the public is not receiving adequate protection against the violent offender under the present sentencing system. I would also require a narrow definition of " crime of violence." Perhaps it should be confined to attempted murder, offences covered by section 18 of the Offences against the Person Act 1861, rape and robbery. Even the mention of robbery gives pause for thought as handbag snatching can easily constitute that crime; but, given the evidence which I have mentioned, and an appropriately restricted definition, I would find it hard to resist the suggestion.

Corrective training. The 1932 Committee on Persistent Offenders recommended that the courts should have power to sentence to detention of from two to four years an offender over twenty-one still in the early stages of a criminal career, in order " to deal with him not merely by inflicting such penalty as is commensurate with his last offence, but by sub-

---

[17] *Walker and Others* [1967] Crim.L.R. 465, reprinted with a critical reply by Dr. Carr Hill in " The Violent Offender: Reality or Illusion," an occasional pamphlet of the Oxford Penology Unit (Basil Blackwell 1970).

jecting him to such treatment as is appropriate to his character." [18] In suitable cases, the sentence would be for training; in others it was to be for the protection of the public. There was, it was thought, a gap which needed to be filled between Borstal training for those under twenty-one, and preventive detention to which it was scarcely likely that any-one under thirty would be sentenced. The upshot was section 21 (1) of the Criminal Justice Act 1948. It provided that, if someone not less than twenty-one was convicted on indictment of an offence punishable with imprisonment for two years or more, he could, provided he had been convicted of such an offence on at least two previous occasions, be sentenced to corrective training of from two to four years. The court had to be satisfied that it was expedient, with a view to the reformation of the offender and the prevention of crime, " that he should receive training of a corrective character for a substantial time, followed by a period of supervision if released before the expiration of his sentence." No reference was made to the possibility of a sentence of comparatively short term detention in excess of that com-mensurate with the gravity of the offence for the protection of the public.

To quote from a leading article on the subject, " The judges' reaction to the new sentence of corrective training was one of enthusiasm soon tempered by some puzzlement." [19] No fewer than 1,106 men and fifty-four women received the sentence in the first six months during which the Act of 1948 was in force; but, not unnaturally, the question was raised as to the manner in which corrective training differed from imprisonment. The honest answer was " not at all," and this

[18] Cmd. 4090, para. 39.
[19] D. J. McClean [1964] Crim.L.R. 745, p. 749.

is in effect what the Prison Commissioners said in their Report of 1949 which stated that it was not the purpose of the Act to provide some new form of training, but to give the courts power to pass sentences long enough to enable methods of training already developed in training prisons to be effectively applied. Nevertheless, the idea that something special was done to offenders sentenced to corrective training persisted to such an extent that, as late as 1962,[20] it was necessary for the Lord Chief Justice to issue a Practice Direction to dispel the illusion that the primary purpose of corrective training was to enable the trainee to learn a trade.

On discovering, as some of them did, that there was no qualitative difference between a sentence of corrective training and a sentence of imprisonment, judges began to flinch at the idea of protracting an offender's sentence to an extent considerably beyond that merited by his offence.[21] On discovering, as many of them no doubt did, that the results of corrective training were, to put it mildly, not very encouraging, the judges ceased to employ the sentence very much. So far as I am aware, no one regretted its abolition by section 37 (1) of the Criminal Justice Act 1967.

Three salutary lessons. I have now completed the sad history of twentieth century English attempts to cope with recidivism. It provides us with at least three salutary lessons.

The first, and far and away the most palatable, is the extreme importance of avoiding calling the same thing by different names. The rather glib memorandum which Paterson submitted to the 1932 Committee on Persistent Offenders contains the following ostensibly challenging statement: " At

[20] [1962] 1 All E.R. 671.
[21] *R.* v. *McCarthy* [1955] 1 W.L.R. 856.

this point, though in truth there may be little in a name but the associations we have built round it, I propose to abolish all prisons—and incidentally, though with some regret, all Prison Commissioners." [22]   The pulp which underlay so much of Paterson's penology is revealed almost immediately. The Prison Commission was to be replaced by a " board of welfare " whose members should, among other things, administer " training centres " and " places of detention." The first " shall be designed for the training of first offenders or of recidivists under some such age as 30, and the last shall retain in custody those who after many efforts and many chances still offend against the law."   The enormous influence of the memorandum can be gauged from the following extract from paragraph 128 of the Committee's Report:

> " If the term penal servitude were abolished there would then be only two designations, namely imprisonment and detention, to describe the two main types of sentence involving the segregation of offenders.   The term imprisonment would cover all ordinary sentences up to life sentences such as are now described by the terms of ' imprisonment ' or ' penal servitude,' and aim primarily at measuring out a term for the offence and in that sense are retributive in character.   The term ' detention ' would cover all sentences which are of a tutelary character and are based on the character of the offender with the object either of subjecting him to reformative training or of detaining him in safe custody for the protection of the public.   Of these tutelary sentences there will be, if our proposals are accepted, three types, namely, Borstal detention, detention for periods of from

[22] *Paterson on Prisons* (ed. Ruck), p. 62.

two to four years and prolonged detention for from four
to ten years."

It is unnecessary for me to dwell on the amount of unnecessary suffering occasioned by this kind of gerrymandering
with words. It is not improbable that some inadequate old
lags received sentences of preventive detention for relatively
innocuous offences because the judge believed that they would
be kept out of circulation in conditions differing considerably
from those of a prison. It is certain that people have received
sentences of corrective training for periods longer than the
prison sentences that they merited because the judge thought
they would be taught a trade. For the offender's reaction to
the discovery that, contrary to what the judge told him, there
was no difference between corrective training and ordinary
imprisonment, it is unnecessary for me to do more than refer
you to Mr. Frank Norman's book, *Bang to Rights*.

The only discriminations which we now make with regard
to incarceration concern the distinctions between imprisonment, detention of children and young persons convicted of
very grave crimes, detention centres and Borstal. At least
these do reflect some differences of treatment, although I am
by no means sure that the Norwegians are not more honest
than we are in calling their equivalent to Borstal a "youth
prison."

The second lesson to be learned from the history which I
have just narrated is the futility of incarcerating offenders
for more protracted periods than are required by the other
demands of criminal justice in order that they may be trained.
Corrective training was the product of the era of penological
optimism. We must now face the fact that, if what is wanted
is training, it had better take place out of prison. We can

no longer delude ourselves into thinking that we are getting the best of both worlds by deterring the offender and others by depriving him of his liberty and, at the same time, training him to lead a useful life. It will be recollected that Paterson indulged in this kind of sophistry with regard to Borstal training.[23] The sophistry is far less defensible in the case of offenders over twenty-one.

The third and most unpalatable lesson to be learned from twentieth century attempts to deal with the recidivists is that we have made no progress whatsoever. Judged by the standard of the number of habitual criminals in and out of our prisons, our system is no better than it was in the days of the Gladstone Report. Recidivism is still the most important of all prison questions, and it certainly remains the most complicated and difficult. Perhaps we have been approaching the problem from the wrong end. We have only attempted to provide for a special sentence and a special prison regime after the offender has become a recidivist. Why should we not concentrate more on the first prison sentence? We constantly remind ourselves of the only pleasing fact we know about our prison system, namely, that some 60 to 70 per cent. of people who serve one sentence do not return to prison. Might it not be as well for the authorities to concentrate their efforts on first prison sentences? If ever there were a time for discussion, advice and offers of help on release, it must surely be the time while an offender is in prison for the first time. If I had my way, the period of his incarceration would be short; ought he not to be given ample opportunity for solitary reflection in his cell by a partial return to the separate system? Should not everything possible be

---

[23] pp. 35–36, *supra*.

done to remind him that the sentence will be longer, and perhaps even tougher, next time, if there is a next time?

2. AN ASSESSMENT OF PENAL REFORM IN TWENTIETH-CENTURY ENGLAND

After the gloom of the first part of this lecture, let us see whether I can do any better with my final assessment of penal reform in twentieth century England. I am committed to the view that a change in the penal system can properly be described as an endeavour to achieve penal reform if it is aimed directly or indirectly at the rehabilitation of the offender, or if its object is to avoid, suspend or reduce punishment on humanitarian grounds. Judged by these criteria, which of the changes I have described in these lectures were endeavours to achieve penal reform, and which of them were successful?

I can give quite a long list in reply to this question, but I must also mention experiments in penal reform that have failed, and the list of successes is subject to one immediate and one possible reservation. The list is as follows: the abolition of capital punishment for murder; the abolition of corporal punishment; the amelioration of prison conditions; the introduction of parole; the introduction of probation; the introduction of the suspended sentence; the prospective abolition of judicial punishment for children under fourteen; and the introduction of special orders to meet the case of the mentally abnormal offender. I have no doubt that I must include preventive detention and corrective training among the experiments in penal reform which have failed; the one aimed at the humane isolation, the other at the reform, of the persistent offender, and each was unsuccessful. I am not sure what I ought to do with regard to Borstal and detention centres. In so far as their aims were rehabilitative, I am afraid they must count as failures; but if they are simply looked upon as improved forms of imprisonment for the seventeen to twenty-one age group, I suppose they could be counted as successes. I realise that the suspended sentence may have to be numbered among the experiments which have failed, an endeavour to keep people out of prison which failed because it was superfluous; but we have not come to that yet.

My immediate reservation is due to the fact that only probation, together with orders to meet the case of the mentally abnormal offender, can be said to be aimed directly or indirectly at rehabilitation. Moreover, it is far from clear that probation has been, or is being, used as an alternative to imprisonment as much as it should be used. Research today suggests that it is about equally effective or ineffective in preventing recidivism, and probation is more humane as well as being much less costly than prison. I suspect that the baneful myth that people could be reformed by protracted imprisonment or some fifteen months' Borstal training has diverted attention from the supremely important endeavour to rehabilitate offenders in the community. At any rate this is the call for the future. There has been progress in penal reform in twentieth-century England if attention is focussed on its humanitarian aspect, but there has not been as much progress as might have been hoped in the rehabilitation of the offender. In many cases this may be an impossible task and the most that can be hoped for may be deterrence by, and isolation in, prison. But it is time we heard more of the training of offenders out of prison and less of training in prison which is so often a euphemism for a dull and inadequate day's work.

The trouble about schemes for rehabilitation in the community is that, unless they are carefully set forth in well planned blueprints, they are apt to bear the appearance of a gimmick. However, it is not asking too much to suggest, as many have recently suggested, that consideration should be given to the formation of community centres, places at which offenders in need of instruction or support could be obliged to attend, during the day if unemployed, in the evenings or over weekends if employed. The attendance could be made the condition of a probation order with imprisonment as the ultimate sanction.

Then there is the possibility of intensive probation. It is highly probable that, if they could be visited by a probation officer or his representative every day, many of the inadequate deviants mentioned in connection with preventive detention would do little serious harm out of prison.

Then there is the possibility of orders for work in the community which, thanks to the report of the Advisory Council on the Penal System on Non-custodial and Semi-custodial Penalties, is under review by the government. The idea is that the offender could be ordered to do so many hours' work in the community during his spare time. His work, such as constructing playgrounds and cleaning up churchyards, would be done in conjunction with the existing voluntary service. It would be arranged by a probation officer and be a condition of probation.

Then there is the possibility of some form of extended hostel system under which offenders who had no proper home could be ordered to live in hostels, paying for their keep with their work, again under the supervision of a probation officer.

Finally, there is the possibility of offenders who are employed being committed to prison from which they would be released for work in the day time.

All the above ideas are, at the moment, a little " half baked." Most of them are dependent on the extension of the probation service to which I referred in my last lecture; but there can be no doubt that we have displayed to date a woeful lack of imagination in the matter of the treatment of offenders. It simply is not good enough for the Home Secretary to say, as he did on June 9, 1971, that " it is better to build on existing and well tried methods rather than to rely too much on wholly new alternatives," and then to give an account of future plans, however desirable they may be, to build new prisons.

My possible reservation with regard to twentieth century penal reform concerns the relaxation of deterrence. I am a believer in penal reform and an optimist. Although I am guessing about matters on which everybody else's guess is as good as mine, I do not think a single change which I have been discussing has reduced the deterrent effect of the threat or experience of punishment to such an extent that it ought to be reversed for that reason; but this is a possibility which every honest penal reformer must be prepared to envisage. For example, I was, and am, an abolitionist on the capital punishment issue, but an abolitionist who had his doubts; one who, being unconvinced either way by the major arguments concerning the uniquely deterrent effect of capital punishment, or the appropriateness or otherwise of taking a life for a life, was led to the abolitionist camp by some rather sophisticated secondary arguments which I have set out elsewhere.[24] I would certainly wish to reconsider my position if

24 Blom Cooper, *The Hanging Question*.

confronted with convincing evidence that a substantial number of criminals would abandon the use of guns if capital punishment for murder were restored. As I am in an unusually honest mood, I should add that the evidence would have to be convincing, that the number of criminals relinquishing the guns would have to be substantial, and that I have only said that I would wish to reconsider my position.

At this point I am minded to stop. After all, these lectures are intended to be an assessment of penal reform in twentieth-century England, and, for what it is worth, I have made my assessment; but I believe that some of the matters I have been discussing raise questions of interest to " common people," who are, in some sense, the beneficiaries of the Hamlyn Trust. I therefore turn to some of those questions, although I regret to say that they will be raised and answered with a brevity that ill becomes a direct beneficiary of Emma Hamlyn's concern with that almost mythical member of our species, the " common man."

3. The Common Man's Questions

It goes without saying that the type of question to be expected from the common man will vary considerably according to his location. Lawyers are wont to place him on the Clapham omnibus. I feel pretty sure that the man on the Clapham omnibus would raise the first three of the questions I am about to mention; but I have reservations about the fourth. There is, however, a sense in which all four questions might be said to come from a member of the " general public," and this accounts in part for the title of these lectures.

Here are the questions. Has there been too much penal reform in twentieth-century England? Is the present punishment for murder as severe as it should be, assuming that there is to be no return to capital punishment? Is adequate consideration given to the victims of crime? Is the idea of personal responsibility declining?

Excessive penal reform. In a sense I have already answered the question whether there has been too much penal reform in twentieth-century England in the negative, for I have said that I do not think any of the changes which I count as penal reform has weakened the deterrent effect of punishment sufficiently to call for its reversal, but a little more in the way of a break up of question and answer does seem to be desirable. The three changes which provoke the question are the abolition of capital punishment for murder, the abolition of corporal punishment and the amelioration of prison conditions.

As to the first, I simply want to say what can be said to allay the common man's very natural fear that, although the abolition of capital punishment may not affect the murder rate, it will lead to an overall increase in crimes of violence simply because a criminal will be less disinclined to use violence as he will not run the risk of being hanged if he murders someone. At a time when crimes of violence are increasing annually, it is impossible to allay this kind of fear by the adduction of evidence; but it is possible to point to certain aspects of the evidence which suggest that the rise in crimes of violence may not be significantly affected by the abolition of capital punishment. Capital punishment for murder was suspended in 1965. Murder can only be committed by someone who intends either to kill or else to cause really serious bodily harm. The greatest increase in reported crimes of violence against the person has taken place in malicious woundings (22,294 in 1966, 35,779 in 1970); these tend to be crimes of the " brawl " variety rather than those committed by the criminal prepared to commit murder. The reported " woundings and other acts endangering life " have also risen, but not so steeply (2,278 in 1966, 2,956 in 1970) and they were actually down on the 1966 figure in 1968. There is also the unpalatable but, I fear, very likely contingency that our society, or at least a substantial part of it, is more violent than it used to be. Allowance must also be made for the low detection rate and the changing pattern of serious crimes like robbery. The efficient mobile gang is likely to use arms, whether or not we have capital punishment, simply because they enhance so greatly the chances of a getaway.

A great many highly speculative and inaccurate statements are made with regard to the deterrent effects of corporal punishment. In answer to the common man's qualms with regard to its abolition, I am content to remind him of the report of the 1938 Committee mentioned in my second lecture,[25] and to beg him to treat assertions that no one was ever flogged twice or old wives' tales about Day J.'s exploits at Liverpool in the 1880s with the contempt they deserve.

There is undoubtedly a body of opinion that the amelioration of prison conditions has taken the bite out of imprisonment for the hardened professional criminal. The suggestion is accordingly made that the courts should be empowered to pass sentences of " rigorous imprisonment " on this type of offender.[26] This is not a proposal to revert to the bad old

[25] p. 61, *supra*.
[26] The suggestion was made by Lawton J. in a memorandum submitted to the Royal Commission on the Penal System 1964–66.

pre-Gladstone days. It is not proposed that prison should be toughened for *all* prisoners, but only for those selected by the courts, and only for those who had already been subjected to ordinary imprisonment. I am not prepared to pronounce on the accuracy of the body of opinion to which I have referred, but I have got some comments to make on the suggestion, although I think it merits serious consideration. If it were adopted there would, *pro tanto*, be a reversal of the trend towards regarding the deprivation of liberty as the punishment which prison entails. I certainly would not regard this as fatal to the suggestion for I have already given my reasons for regarding Paterson's aphorism that people are sent to prison *as* and not *for* punishment as no more than a half truth [27]; but the implementation of the suggestion would be retrogressive. Those who advocate " rigorous imprisonment " contemplate conditions of lots of hard work and little association; the extent to which it would be possible to plan such a regime compatibly with the demands of humanity and the preservation of a reasonable staff-prisoner relationship is another matter. But the thing which worries me most about the proposal is the question of selection. Is it the case that every judge knows a hardened professional criminal fit for rigorous imprisonment when he sees one? The history of the prison divisions and preventive detention raises doubts about the merits of the courts as selectors of suitable criminals for special kinds of incarceration; and, if " rigorous imprisonment " were to be the severe deterrent that its sponsors have in mind, it would surely be wrong to vest in the Home Secretary any power of transferring offenders to or from it.

[27] p. 33, *supra.*

Sentence for murder. As the sentence for murder is currently under consideration by the Criminal Law Revision Committee, the less I say about its adequacy the better. The present punishment is a life sentence which the court must impose and it differs from other life sentences because, under the Murder (Abolition of Death Penalty) Act 1965, the trial judge has power to declare the minimum period which, in his view, should elapse before the Home Secretary exercises his power of releasing the offender on licence. As in the case of every other life sentence, the Home Secretary can only release the murderer on licence on the recommendation of the Parole Board, and after consultation with the Lord Chief Justice together with the trial judge if he is available.

I suspect that the common man's fears come from what he has read about lifers being released after they have served eight or nine years of their sentences. He is disposed to attribute the following line of reasoning to the armed robber. " If I kill the man who is pursuing me and I am caught, I shall be convicted of murder and should be out after eight or nine years. I would get as much as that for the robbery. Therefore, I will commit murder and reduce the risk of being caught." But this reasoning would be fallacious. None of us knows what practice will be adopted either by the Home Office or by the Parole Board with regard to recommendations under the Act of 1965. Six recommendations for as much as thirty years have been made already. The recommendation is not subject to appeal, there is no inbred system of remission after two-thirds, or parole after a third. If the Home Secretary accepts these thirty-year recommendations to the full, the offenders will have served the equivalent of a fixed-term sentence of forty-five years on which full remission, but no parole was granted, something as yet unheard of in this country. Surely this is a case for " let us wait and see." The desirability of such a course is enhanced by the reflection that, in a case like that which I have just contemplated, it is now possible for a court to pass a fixed-term sentence for the robbery together with a life sentence for the murder. Precisely how the Home Office or the Parole Board will react when confronted with such sentences is anybody's guess.

The Victim. The question whether adequate considera-tion is given to the victims of crime is liable to reveal the difference of approach of the lawyer from that of the common man. The lawyer is apt to say that compensation is the concern of the civil law and punishment the concern of the criminal law; if the spectacle of the punishment of the criminal causes the victim pleasure, all well and good; but it would certainly be wrong for there to be any closer relation-ship between the punishment and the views of the victim. The common man is wont to point to occasions on which he has seen or heard of the offender being put on probation for some nefarious crime which was plainly worthy of condign punishment. Matters are not made any better, in the eye of the common man, if the court has addressed the criminal at length and said nothing whatever to or of the victim in whose wound the iron is turned still further by the sight of the criminal raising his hat to him on leaving the court.[28]

The common man would therefore approve of the state-ment in paragraphs 24 and 25 of " Penal Practice in a Changing Society " that a fundamental re-examination of penal methods should consider, not only the obligations of

[28] See a letter to *The Times*, August 21, 1971.

society and the offender to one another, but also the obligations of both to the victim.

> " The assumption that the claims of the victim are sufficiently satisfied if the offender is punished by society becomes less persuasive as society in its dealings with offenders increasingly emphasizes the reformative aspects of punishment. Indeed in the public mind the interests of the offender may not infrequently seem to be placed before those of his victim. This is certainly not the correct emphasis."

Obviously the common man cannot expect legislation decreeing that judges should always say nice things about victims and nasty things about offenders, but he can ask what tangible provision is made for the compensation of the victim. To this the answer is a fairly heartening one. Although Great Britain was just beaten to the post by New Zealand in 1964, we can claim to be among the first countries in the world to have made general provision for compensation by the state for personal injuries sustained in consequence of crime. Admittedly the scheme only provides for *ex gratia* payments, and sometimes the victim will not do as well under the scheme as he would under a satisfied judgment in a civil action; but one only has to consult the six reports of the Criminal Injuries Compensation Board in order to see that society is doing something for the victims of crime. There are several reasons why the scheme should not apply to damage to and loss of property. The risk of fraudulent claims would be far greater than it is in the case of personal injuries, and the outlay would probably require some kind of general contributory insurance scheme; but, if we really want to have public confidence in some of the schemes for the treatment of criminals

in the community to which I have referred, it may be necessary to extend the present scheme for compensation by the
State to offences against property. It goes without saying that
the scheme would, like the present one, have to be subject to
stringent conditions about reporting and so forth.

Civil claims against the offender himself are always
possible, though rare; orders for restitution and compensation
may be made under various statutes, but these again are not
made in every case, simply because of the obvious unlikeli-
hood of their being complied with, although the Court of
Appeal has recently made short shrift of an argument that an
order for compensation should not be made under the
Forfeiture Act 1870 against someone sent to prison because
the necessity of complying with it might impede his rehabilitation after release.[29] A report of the Advisory Council on
the Penal System published in 1970 recommended experimentation with a scheme of criminal bankruptcy whereby,
in cases in which the claim of the victim was substantial, the
courts might fix its amount, and treat the conviction as an
act of bankruptcy. It is anybody's guess how this scheme
will work. The government are also considering the possibility of empowering the courts to defer sentences and release
an offender on bail, in order, among other things, to see
whether he takes steps to make restitution.

Is there anything else that could be done? What about
this suggestion relating to acquisitive crimes, theft, obtaining
by deception and the like?

" Let the prisoner be required to disclose what he has
done with his booty. And if he refuses or fails to satisfy

[29] *R.* v. *Ironfield* [1971] 1 All E.R. 200n.

the court that it is out of his power to do so, let there be but one sentence—imprisonment for life." [30]

These words come from a book which met with the almost fulsome commendation of Wills J.[31] Of course I can see objections to the proposal, but it merits consideration, and I certainly do not think that it should be turned down because of the impropriety of bargaining with the criminal. We must not let ourselves be enslaved by some kind of primitive instinct against compounding a crime, particularly now that it is no longer an offence to compound a felony.

Responsibility. This is no place for a discussion of the meaning attached by the common man to such expressions as " personal responsibility." I shall assume that, when he asks whether the idea of personal responsibility is declining, he means that someone is personally responsible for his criminal acts or omissions when he can properly be punished for them according to law, and that the more excuses that are allowed, the more the idea of personal responsibility is on the decline: I also assume that there is the implication that this is a bad thing. My reply to the common man's question, thus understood, is that there has been a decline in the idea of personal responsibility, but this is no bad thing. Obvious instances of the decline are changes in the law with regard to the criminal responsibility of the immature and mentally abnormal; but allowance should no doubt also be made for an increase in the number of commonly accepted mitigating circumstances such as the poor social background of the offender, or the pressures which beset him. A lawyer would

[30] Anderson, *Criminals and Crime*, p. 27 (Nesbet & Co. 1907).
[31] *The Nineteenth Century and After*, Vol. LXII, p. 879.

say that this is a matter which affects the quantity of punishment rather than criminal responsibility; I suspect, however,
that the common man's retort would be that this is just one
more example of legal pedantry.

The increase in the age of criminal responsibility from
seven to ten is an instance of the decline of personal responsibility because it augmented a class which is totally excused.
The same can be said of the complete exemption from
punishment of children between the ages of ten and fourteen
for crimes other than homicide contemplated by the Children
and Young Persons Act 1969, although, as we have seen, the
question of criminal responsibility will still have to be considered in care proceedings. The restrictions on the punishment of young persons between the ages of fourteen and
seventeen tend in the same direction. I have already given
my reasons for regarding judicial punishment as too blunt an
instrument in the case of children under fourteen, and, though
I must admit that there is more room for debate here, I have
suggested that nothing much will be lost if it ceases to be
possible to send boys between the ages of fourteen and
seventeen to a detention centre, or young persons of either
sex between the ages of fifteen and seventeen to Borstal.

As to the mentally abnormal offender, a lawyer would
say that the development during this century of the court's
powers to make what are now called hospital or guardianship
orders does not affect responsibility because the courts remain
free to punish the offender if they are so minded. I am not
sure what the common man would say to that. He would
probably allege pedantry again, but he might take my view
that, however proper it may be to send the mentally ill to
prison for security reasons, it is certainly wrong to imprison
them for the sake of punishment. The lawyer and the com-

mon man would agree that the introduction of the defence of diminished responsibility by the Homicide Act 1957 can be said to mark a further decline in the idea of personal responsibility because it enables someone who is guilty of murder because he intended to kill, or cause really serious bodily harm to, his victim, and who cannot plead insanity to " get away with " a verdict of manslaughter.

So far as England and Wales are concerned, the defence of diminished responsibility, borrowed from Scots law, owes its existence to the narrowness of the McNaghten Rules and the persistence of capital punishment. Under the McNaghten Rules, a plea of insanity can only succeed if the accused can prove that he was suffering from a defect of reason due to disease of the mind which prevented him from knowing the nature and quality of his act, or, if he did know that much, from knowing that it was wrong. Very soon after their formulation, the point was taken that they made no allowance for cases of impaired self-control due to mental illness. Sir James Stephen who, as we saw in my second lecture, was no opponent of the idea of punishment, thought that the McNaghten Rules did cover such a case, but his views were not accepted by the English courts. In 1924, a Committee presided over by Lord Atkin recommended the addition of a clause which would allow for the defence of impaired self-control, somewhat unfortunately described as " irresistible impulse "; but this proved unacceptable to Parliament. The Royal Commission on Capital Punishment of 1949–53 was divided. One member, need I say that he was a lawyer, favoured the *status quo*. Three members were in favour of adding a clause according to which, if the jury are satisfied that the accused knew the nature and quality of his act, and that it was wrong, they must still acquit him if satisfied that he was incapable of preventing himself from committing the act. The majority of the Commission would have gone further; they favoured the total abolition of the McNaghten Rules. They suggested that one broad question should be left to the jury, namely, whether at the time of the act, the accused was suffering from a disease of the mind or mental deficiency to such a degree that he ought not to be held responsible. No action was taken on this recommendation, but, as part of a last ditch compromise over the issue of capital punishment, section 2 of the Homicide Act 1957 provides that a person who kills another shall not be convicted of murder if he was suffering from such abnormality of mind as substantially impaired his mental responsibility for his acts and omissions in doing or being a party to the killing. A verdict of manslaughter must be returned in cases falling within section 2 with the result that the court has a complete discretion with regard to the sentence.

Capital punishment for murder has been abolished, the McNaghten Rules are obsolescent in the sense that reliance is very seldom placed upon them, and section 2 of the Homicide Act is still in force. Is this a satisfactory state of affairs? I certainly cannot endorse the following breathtaking statement to be found in a book which was presumably meant for the common man, " The McNaghten Rules are the distillation of the accumulated wisdom of centuries of judicial practice. It is thanks to them in part at any rate if we sleep as safe and sound in our beds as we do." [32] All the same it is arguable that, although England is behind most other countries in refusing to allow for seriously impaired self-control due to mental illness in its general insanity defence, things work well enough in practice. Allowance is made for

[32] F. T. Giles, *Children and the Law*, pp. 87–88 (Penguin Books. 1959).

seriously impaired self-control in murder cases by means of the defence of diminished responsibility [33]; and, in all other cases, it can be reflected in the sentence. Where the offender is mentally ill at the time of conviction, a hospital or guardianship order can be made; where he is not mentally ill at the time of conviction, he can, in a proper case, be discharged or put on probation and, if the case is one of diminished responsibility, there is, perhaps, no objection to a period of imprisonment which may, in the interests of public security, sometimes have to be for life. I realise, however, that there are moral objections to convicting someone of any crime, not only when he did not know what he was doing or that it was wrong, but also when, for some other reason, he was prevented by mental illness from conforming to the law. I also realise that it is well nigh impossible to find any basis on which allowance can be made for diminished responsibility in calculating the appropriate quantity of punishment. It is arguable that the case should be one of all or nothing. I therefore feel constrained on theoretical grounds to advocate the adoption in this country of the following provisions of the American Law Institute's Model Penal Code.

"§ 4.01 (i) A person is not responsible for criminal conduct if at the time of such conduct as a result of mental disease or defect he lacks substantial capacity either to appreciate the criminality [wrongfulness] of his conduct or to conform his conduct to the requirements of the law."

This would render the defence of diminished responsibility otiose. Someone acquitted of any crime, including murder, on the ground of insanity would, as now, be liable to deten-

---

[33] *R.* v. *Byrne* [1960] 2 Q.B. 396.

tion at Her Majesty's pleasure. I have described my grounds for advocating the adoption of this clause as theoretical because I doubt very much whether it would add greatly to the number of cases in which the insanity defence is raised. I think paragraph 4.01 preferable to the majority recommendation of our Royal Commission simply because it is less vague.

I cannot refrain from quoting sub-clause 2: " As used in this article the terms ' mental disease or defect ' do not include an abnormality manifested only by repeated criminal or otherwise anti-social conduct." This hits at Lady Wootton's *bête noire,* the psychopath, or rather at what she regards as the way in which psychiatrists are wont to seek to prove psychopathy.

This brings us back to the question of the extent to which the whole institution of punishment has been eroded by, or needs to be adapted to, new beliefs about the human mind, so provocatively raised by Professor Hart.[34]

My attempt to cope with the common man's qualm about the decline in the idea of personal responsibility has shown that there has been erosion in the case of the immature and the mentally abnormal. There has also been erosion at other points. We do not regard punishment as by any means the necessary consequence of a conviction of crime; we are less sure than our nineteenth century forebears that someone not demonstrably mentally ill was as free from pressures to commit crimes as we believe ourselves to be; and we believe more than they did in the possibility of rehabilitation in the community. With these reservations, however, it would be wholly wrong to suggest that there has been anything in the nature of a complete erosion of the

[34] p. 54, *supra.*

institution of punishment. It is fitting that Ruggles-Brise should be given the last word, so far as these lectures are concerned:

> " You cannot expel human nature with a fork, and moral indignation against the perpetrator of an anti-social act is in human nature, and will demand certainty and fixity of punishment where there is full responsibility for the deed." [35]

4. Incidental Suggestions

It is customary for lecturers and writers on controversial legal topics to conclude with a summary of their proposals for reform, but I have not regarded my present mission as one of reform so much as of assessment, and I would therefore like the following summary to be regarded as one of suggestions for consideration incidentally thrown out in the course of these lectures. I hope I have made it clear that I am not wedded to by any means all of them; I simply think they should be considered. It follows that I am not in the least perturbed by the fact that some of them are mutually inconsistent. Moreover, I am aware that some of them are superlatively unimportant.

The following are the suggestions I have thrown out—

(1) Remission of all prison sentences involving incarceration for four years or more, *i.e.* sentences of six years or more, should be on licence.

(2) The second and subsequent parole reviews of prisoners serving sentences of ten years or more should not be

[35] *Prison Reform at Home and Abroad*, p. 160.

annual, but should be at dates to be fixed after the previous review.

(3) The length of sentence currently imposed for periods of three years or less should be reduced.

(4) Though it is recognised that this may be impossible in the case of serious offences tried by higher courts, a first prison sentence should not, in general, be more than three months. Because this sentence is so important, every consideration should be given to means of preventing recidivism at this stage. Consideration should also be given to the proposal that the courts should be empowered to pass a special sentence of " rigorous imprisonment " on hardened professional criminals.

(5) There should be no fixed-term sentences of more than ten or fourteen years; but the possibility of empowering the judge to recommend a minimum period of incarceration in the case of all life sentences should be considered.

(6) Everything should be done to encourage a very great increase in the probation and after-care service, and the possibility of encouraging the avoidance of imprisonment by means of orders for attendance at community centres or work in the community should be fully considered.

(7) The courts should be required to give reasons for not suspending a first, or possibly any, prison sentence. The provisions for mandatory suspension should be repealed.

(8) The rebuttable presumption of innocence of a child between the ages of ten and fourteen, and the con-

clusive presumption that a boy of fourteen is incapable of sexual intercourse should be abolished.

(9) The sooner the Children and Young Persons Act 1969 is made fully operative the better.

(10) The courts should be empowered to pass fixed-term custodial sentences on young offenders between the ages of seventeen and twenty-one, as in the case of older offenders; the only difference being that the Executive should have power to decide where the sentence should be spent (detention centre, prison, or Borstal) and the Executive should have power to release at any time.

(11) The courts should cease to impose punitive sentences in cases covered by section 60 of the Mental Health Act 1959; and consideration should be given to the adoption of paragraph 4.01 of the American Law Institute's Model Penal Code.

(12) Consideration should be given to obliging the courts to pass long sentences in the case of offences of repeated violence.

(13) In the case of offences against property, consideration should be given to the possibility of threatening the offender with an increased sentence if he does not disclose the whereabouts of the property he had obtained.

(14) Assuming that there is to be no return to capital punishment, the present rules with regard to the sentence for murder should be retained.

5. THE ROYAL COMMISSION ON THE PENAL SYSTEM 1964–66

Who should do the considering in the case of the above incidental suggestions, and the numerous other more significant proposals that are made from time to time? For my part, I am more than content to leave that to the Advisory Council on the Penal System, but I have yet to complete the tale of the proposal for a thorough review of the whole system originally contemplated in Penal Practice in a Changing Society.

This White Paper was followed by another, " The War Against Crime " published in 1964. In it the opinion was expressed that the time had come for the fundamental review mentioned five years earlier. The appointment of a Royal Commission was proposed, and its terms of reference stated. The Commission was duly appointed in August 1964, under the chairmanship of Lord Amory, but, after some of its members had expressed a wish to resign, it was dissolved in April 1966. Four volumes of the evidence submitted to and taken by the Commission have been published, so there is a sense in which it can be said that the entire operation was not a vain one. All the same, one can but be tempted to inquire into its failure. One obvious reason was a change of government, and I do not say that with any *arrières pensées* concerning party politics. The point is that, by April 1966, the government's plans for the very important and all-embracing Bill which later became the Criminal Justice Act 1967 were already far advanced; the White Papers entitled " The Adult Offender " and " The Child the Family and the Young Offender " had already been published and were the subjects of keen debate. I can, however, think of two other reasons for the failure of the Amory Commission, although they are so closely connected that they should be regarded as one. The first is that, throughout the nineteenth and twentieth centuries, such progress as has been made with regard to penal methods has not been made in consequence of an " overall look," but as the result of a specific reference. Could there be a better example of this than the Gladstone Report? The second of the two further reasons for the failure of the Amory Commission which I have just mentioned is the extreme breadth of the terms of reference. They were as follows:

" In the light of the modern knowledge of crime and its causes and of modern penal practice here and abroad, to consider the conditions and purposes which should underlie the punishment and treatment of offenders in England and Wales: to report how far they are realized by the penalties and methods of treatment available to the courts and whether any changes in these or in the arrangements and responsibility for selecting the sentences to be imposed on the particular offenders are desirable: to review the work of the services and institutions dealing with the offenders and responsibility for their administration and to make recommendations."

I am content to leave the consideration of the incidental suggestions which I have made to the Advisory Council, partly on account of the excellence of its reports to date, but also on account of the great suitability of an inquiry into prison discipline and the principles underlying prison sentencing following upon an inquiry into the treatment of young offenders. In fact, one might say, now that the plans for the treatment of children and young persons have been settled by the Children and Young Persons Act 1969, the next step is a report, already in hand, by the Advisory

Council on the subject of offenders between the ages of seventeen and twenty-one. It seems only right that the step after that should be a report by the Council on prison conditions and sentencing. The original terms of reference of the Gladstone Committee related to prison conditions; this did not prevent the Committee's Report from containing within its interstices statements of principle which were to operate as guide lines for seventy years to come. The same sort of thing could happen now. My final message is that, no matter what the source may be (Advisory Council, Departmental Committee, Inter-departmental Committee or Royal Commission) we want another Gladstone Report.

SELECTED BIBLIOGRAPHY

THE following books dealing with some of the subjects covered by the lectures should be of interest to the general reader.

ANON, *Five Years Penal Servitude by One who has Done It* (1877).

BLOM COOPER, L. (editor), *The Hanging Question* (1969).

BROCKLEHURST, F., *I was in Prison* (1898).

CROSS, R., *The English Sentencing System* (1971).

DU CANE, E., *The Punishment and Prevention of Crime* (1885).

EWING, A. C., *The Morality of Punishment* (1929).

FOX, L., *English Prisons and Borstals* (1952).

HART, H. L. A., *Punishment and Responsibility* (1968).

HOBHOUSE and BROCKWAY, *English Prisons Today* (1921).

HOOD, R., *Borstal Reassessed* (1965).

KLARE, H., *The Anatomy of Prison* (1960).

LESLIE, SHANE, *Sir Evelyn Ruggles-Brise* (1938).

PARKER, TONY, *The Frying Pan* (1970).

ROSE, G., *The Struggle for Penal Reform* (1961).

RUCK, S. K. (editor), *Paterson on Prisons* (1951).

RUGGLES-BRISE, E., *The English Prison System* (1921).

RUGGLES-BRISE, E., *Prison Reform at Home and Abroad* (1924).

WALKER, N., *Crime and Punishment in Great Britain* (1970) (second revised reprint).

WALKER, N., *Sentencing in a Rational Society* (1969).

WEBB, S. and B., *English Prisons Under Local Government* (1922).

WOOTTON, B., *Crime and the Criminal Law* (1963).

The following are the principal Stationery Office publications mentioned in the lectures. Several of them are out of print.

Report of the Departmental Committee on Prisons 1895, Cmd. 7703 (the Gladstone Report).

Report of the Departmental Committee on the Treatment of Young Offenders 1927, Cmd. 2831 (the Moloney Report).

Report of the Departmental Committee on Persistent Offenders 1932, Cmd. 4090 (the Dove Wilson Report).

Report of the Departmental Committee on Corporal Punishment 1938, Cmd. 5684 (the Cadogan Report).

Hubert and East, *The Psychological Treatment of Crime.*

Report of the Royal Commission on Capital Punishment 1953, Cmd. 8932 (the Gowers Report).

Penal Practice in a Changing Society 1959, Cmd. 645.

Report of the Advisory Council on the Treatment of Offenders on Corporal Punishment 1960.

Report of the Advisory Council on the Treatment of Offenders on Preventive Detention 1963.

The War Against Crime 1959–64, Cmd. 2296.

The Adult Offender 1965, Cmd. 2852.

The Child the Family and the Young Offender 1965, Cmd. 2742.

Children in Trouble 1968, Cmd. 3601.[1]

People in Prison 1969, Cmd. 4214.

Report of the Advisory Council on the Penal System on Non-custodial and Semi-custodial Penalties 1970.

---

[1] This White Paper is not mentioned in the lectures, but it is essential reading as the corollary to "The Child the Family and the Young Offender," and as the basis of the Children and Young Persons Act 1969.